Get There First

JOE BOROI

Copyright © 2018 Joe Boroi

All rights reserved.

ISBN-10: 1726029433
ISBN-13: 978-1726029438

DEDICATION

Katie & Addison

CONTENTS

Change is hard..2
Be Bold..20
Be Informed...38
Shape Opportunity..49
Provide Guidance...63
Build Trust...79
Establish Partnership..91
Measure Results..107
Inspire Courage...129

ACKNOWLEDGMENTS

Special thanks to Paul Costianes, David Cantwell, Duane Meaux, Pat Duncan, Dan Gade, Rich Laughlin, and Tom Maher.

Get There First

Joe Boroi

Change is hard

Let's face it, change is hard. It's jarring and disruptive. It's obscure, unpredictable, and unproven. When we face the impossible or navigate the unknown, it's hard to know whether we are on the right path. Making the right decision in the dark is difficult. Influencing or leading others to do so is even harder. Yet, changes in the environment and the fog of a situation are unavoidable. We follow our instinct and stick to our beliefs and values to help us through.

Thousands of years ago, humans erected some of the earliest megaliths. The structures and carvings that they left behind for us to discover indicate that very early on, we built a complex human society. The people who built many of the earliest megaliths chose to depict some rather imposing creatures in their stone monuments. They erected massive carvings of lions, snakes, spiders, and scorpions.

These people decided to illustrate predators on their stone structures instead of the game that they themselves hunted. For whatever reason, some of the earliest human societies went to great lengths so that they could portray the animals that were a danger to human beings. Was it a reminder of the everyday threats that these early people faced? Was it perhaps a record so that future generations wouldn't have to navigate the unknown? Whatever it was, one thing about these stone megaliths is certain. Since the dawn of civilization, humans have had to face threats in their environment. These threats left a lasting impression on each generation. We may not know where danger will find us, but, we do know it's out there.

Facing the unknown is just a fact of life. We all face unfamiliar situations each day in one form or another. There is always a need to change or evolve some aspect of our life. To get by, we follow our gut and rely on the support of others. We push forward despite the roadblocks that are encountered along the way.

Advancements in science and technology are constantly shaking our assumptions about the world. Our reality is evolving and changing every day. Our cultural norms and expectations are changing too. It would be impossible for anyone to comprehend what certain technologies might look like in the future. One generation might share information in exchange for access to lower cost products and services, whereas, another generation might isolate themselves to feel more secure. How an investment in security might eventually manifest itself into more transparency is any one's guess. It's hard to imagine how actions in a given moment can have the opposite effect we are targeting over the long term.

For example, people might allow beacons and listening devices in their homes to improve communication, access content, and lower the cost of utilities. Decades before, this same type of technology would have felt threatening and invasive. Yet, the same research that made these devices more secure also improved them in other ways too.

The environment, conditions, and needs of society changed. The devices, in turn, became smaller, mobile, more marketable, and interconnected. In the past, people would have shunned the idea that big brother might be listening or watching them. Later, they accepted this as a tradeoff for access to other technologies that improved their life in one way or another. Our values and beliefs change. As technology advances, new ways of communicating, sharing, or collaborating will take shape. When change like this occurs, our social contract is re-written based on the conditions or expectations of a generation.

Today, we value a more open and transparent world. The fear of who might be listening has slowly faded away. Society has traded security for wide scale adoption of a more convenient method of communicating at great distances. As our technologies evolve further, this acceptance or bias toward transparency could change once again. We might value isolationism and privacy as the next wave of technology hits or we might find a balance in how our existing technology can complement the need for safety.

Either way, the future is in many ways un-predictable. We conceptualize and forecast it based on what we think we know today. It's the context of the time that matters. A solution that is less than optimal in a certain time and place could be the next best thing as conditions change in the environment.

For an idea to make sense, we must first understand the situation and the environment in which it exists. People recycle old ideas when conditions evolve. Often, new ideas, are based on a long existing hypothesis. The impossible becomes possible when the conditions improve. The wind of progress can gain momentum when just a few variables in the environment shift. It often doesn't take much to spark the wind of change. Our societies aren't always prepared but as individuals, we can be, if we remain objective and adaptable.

Sometimes, progress outpaces our ability to keep up with change. Most periods deemed as a revolution or renaissance in human history are quickly followed by periods of social upheaval and change. When this happens, our social and political systems are tested. Our new reality is strained by the carryover from our old one. This is the debt we incur as a species. Human progress and evolution creates social debt. We carry this debt collectively. Some are left behind by change. The choices we make in the short term catch up with us over the long term.

Social debt is hard to manage collectively and even harder to get past individually when we feel left behind. We try desperately to make sense of things. We work hard to try and get along. We don't always get it right, but we keep trying. We rely on leaders to help us move in a common direction. Our leaders keep us honest. In the past, leaders were individuals. In the future, humanity will continue to evolve its collective conscious.

Technology will allow us to collaborate and influence without clearly designated leaders. Eventually, we might come close to processing information and acting in real time as one organism. That reality is a distant one. We value our individual liberty and will continue to fight to ensure that freedom prevails within the collective conscious. These two things will need to find balance. Just as there was a bloody road behind us, there will be a bloody road ahead. Humanity will struggle to balance liberty and collective consciousness in a world where every device collects, shares, and actuates data on a scale that is beyond human comprehension. We will fight our old battles in the context of a new situation or environment.

In the near term, we will continue to see groups that form movements that work together and act without a formal leader at the helm. Organizations are constantly testing new ways of self-organizing. Teams within teams that organize themselves to be self-sufficient can simultaneously become both a whole and a part within a system. These types of self-organizing groups are self-reliant and can handle contingencies without authority or instruction. Yet, at the same time, a team is always subjected to some form of control from one or more higher authorities.

A holarchy is a hierarchy of self-regulating teams that function autonomously, while controlled or governed by the contextual rules of a situation, and in coordination with an environment. As technology evolves to support the holarchy, people will form groups and organizations that are self-reliant yet organized and influenced toward an objective.

This sort of individual, yet, collective conscious will have many of the same challenges any group organism would, but, perhaps, on a scale that is hard to understand today. Leaderless organizations may come together to change social injustices and at the same time they may also form to commit social injustices.

We will indeed see groups fight each other in a leaderless world where collective thought could aimlessly evolve and threaten peace or prosperity around the world. This may seem like a dark future, but, there is hope. Hope, that, we will work past these challenges, and a new generation of human leaders will emerge to take on and tackle these challenges of governing our collective decision engines. There is hope that we will balance order and chaos in this new world.

Self-organization relies on the throughput of energy and matter. It needs to be fueled with purpose, people, and resources. Self-organizing teams exist at a balance between order and chaos. A shift too far in either direction becomes their undoing. Collective activity will always have the potential for independent action at any given moment. Humanity may never discover a true collective conscious, but, we will indeed find ourselves influenced by the need to work together toward a common goal.

We will also learn in due time that our collective conscious is just as dangerous as any poor leader or dictator found in history. It can be corrupted and fixed by the rules and weights that throttle or control its algorithms. When this happens, it will be a difficult lesson to learn.

We know from history that poor leaders can create unimaginable destruction and chaos in the world. Our collective conscious is no different. We will face the same challenges and more with this new form of leadership. Until technology allows our collective aspirations to reach a state of enlightenment, we will disrupt it and adapt it. It will take people to do this. It will also take people to defend our individual liberties and rights in a world where the benefits of collectivism can feel as if they outweigh the potential oppression of group conscious.

Social debt and the liabilities of our technology or progress are not new ideas. We have been dealing with these things on some level since the dawn of humanity. Most of our world's religions have constructs that are based around some of these ideas. We have sensed and prepared ourselves for this duality. Leaders will influence new communities of people in the coming centuries to tackle many of these challenges in the same ways that we always have. In the workplace, the market, our homes, schools, or our government, these leaders will form new teams and influence those around them.

No matter how complex the world gets, our truth continues to be a mix of old and new ideas. Today's philosophers and thinkers face many of the same challenges or questions that have existed for centuries. They might feel different or sound different today, but, when you look closely, you will see the same pattern or compounded truths. Our assumptions may change but often the foundation by which we see or measure the world rarely does.

As humans, we only have so many senses. There is a finite spectrum by which we can interpret or process our environment. Our physical abilities are limited as well. There are only so many ways we can actuate on what our senses learn. Then, there is the construct of time and space. Time limits us further in this world. There is only so much time and so much room for us to work together. Yet, despite these limitations, humanity finds a way. We constantly expand on the truth, test boundaries, push beyond limits, and augment our abilities. We form teams to tackle the most difficult of challenges. We do all of this to try and overcome any problem. Together, we partner and influence each other to rethink what might be possible. We adapt, and we disrupt.

Therefore, our complex world needs disruptive leaders with a solid and objective understanding of what is around them. Teams need to focus and pay attention to their environment. Yet, the disruptive leader also needs to understand that our changing world demands quite a bit of flexibility to adapt and overcome the unknown.

Often an organization is left helplessly in the dark and may not know what is beyond a team's immediate field of vision. Leaders must anticipate less than ideal conditions for execution. It's easy for a leader to let obstacles get the best of them. Disruptive leaders must help their team focus so that they aren't lost or held back by a lack of detail.

On the other hand, a tidal wave of oncoming variables or an open ocean of potential solutions can paralyze a team just as easily. Sometimes, too much information or too many conflicting data points can make it just as difficult to decide what's next.

In today's world, our machines use predictive insights and complex matching algorithms to orchestrate rules, associations, and meta-data. This data stream is sourced from an endless array of sensing capabilities in the environment around us. Technologies can help teams make decisions with less time, money, and effort. These same tools also help leaders influence communities on a massive scale.

In this way, technology doesn't replace our humanity. It enhances who we are and what we are capable of. It gives us strength and new-found abilities. Leaders and teams that rely on technologies to assist them, consume machine-driven recommendations so that they have a much shorter list of solutions to choose from or variables to process.

Those that share information in this sort of an ecosystem then have a much easier time engaging and partnering in the world. Decisions are easier, faster, and cheaper. Our external relationships are different but stronger and more intimate.

Change is never easy. It often results in conflict and new philosophical understandings. Our beliefs are challenged and our assumptions or attitudes toward the world are rocked by a new experience. From the ashes of progress, a new city state emerges where our lives are an open book and human or system interaction is a constant real-time exchange of value across a virtualized integrated network.

What feels like a win-win on the outside comes with a dangerous trade-off. Data sharing, curation, reporting, and decisioning capabilities often become a black box for a team. This means that they don't understand how new tools or capabilities make decisions and recommendations. They blindly trust and rely on the information but fail to realize or understand whether it has been compromised. Leaders and teams can become confused and disoriented by corrupted or bias information. It may also mean, alternatively, that they don't trust the tool as designed and have abandoned it all together. In either case, the team may become aimless and unable to adapt.

The golden rule of personalized data is to collect it overtly and share it covertly. This means that most individuals don't even realize or understand how they are being influenced every day. We begin to rely on technology and accept it at face value never questioning the cost or intent behind certain aspects of our devices and user experiences.

In a world where data is shared regularly, leaders often stop thinking about or considering where the data comes from or how it is orchestrated. They put trust in a system in exchange for leverage. Teams accept what they are told. Leaders stop thinking about what is real or what else might be possible. All these things open the door to groups that are hoping to influence with false or misleading data. The disruptive leader hedges their bet, takes advantage of these capabilities, but remains skeptical and vigilant.

Being skeptical doesn't require leaders or teams to abandon technology. Instead, they should work toward understanding it to ensure that it is not corrupted. This also means that leaders must be sure that the team is using it correctly. All too often, teams will abandon technology or process because they believe it was doing them wrong. The reality though is that the technology was used incorrectly, the data was miss-interpreted, or the process miss-used. Poor leaders dismiss a technology or process all together. Individuals who immediately dismiss any idea have often weighted their own experience, bias, or attitudes so that they can't accept new thoughts or ideas. Their hypothesis of a situation is already optimized to a point that they can no longer accept a new idea or alternate reality.

Disruptive leaders recognize that optimized information can make a team short sided or complacent. In this scenario, the most likely decisions become the only decision. This also means that the most relevant content becomes the only content a team uses to understand or communicate.

Disruptive leaders are not only objective but contradictive. They can love what they hate and hate what they love. They see value in all sides of an equation. These leaders look beyond the obvious and actively seek out information that others are ignoring. They see patterns from the outside as much as they do the inside of an organization.

Disruptive leaders understand that, to be effective, teams and individuals need to be free thinkers and thought leaders in their craft. Tools and capabilities can help inform their decisions, provide relevant contextual information, or automate a process, but, they should never replace free will. We are all influenced by the fractal circumstances of our environment and situation. Disruptive leaders remain open minded and adaptive despite what they think or believe in a given moment.

Get There First

To make quick and decisive decisions, leaders must have an acute ability to listen. They can't allow themselves or the team to be distracted by the noise or chaos around them. With the outcome in mind, great leaders know how to measure their success and failure so that the team can adapt and overcome.

The team must learn and grow with every new experience. Great leaders are never afraid of a new opportunity. They welcome challenges and embrace them. This sort of optimism isn't always easy, and it can come at a price. Sometimes individuals or teams get out ahead of the pack and then become isolated and alone. That is why partnership is critical. Partners increase a leader's confidence and provide the team with a sense of security when they have wandered too far ahead of an organization.

None of us can take on the world alone. We need to collaborate with those around us to survive. Our humanity is not just found in our individualism. Our collectivism plays a role in who we are or aspire to be. Each of us seeks to balance our individual liberty with our collective commitment to one and other. Too much of either can prove to be fatal in this world. Aligning to a common goal can form the bedrock of a solid partnership or the binding of our collective fabric. Leaders understand this, and so they push teams to unite under common interests.

As human communication platforms and methods expand through various technological advancements, it becomes easier and easier for teams to form new and exciting partnerships. However, self-organization across new territories can fall into the same trap as data sharing and personalization. It can be corrupted and falsely influenced by forces in the environment.

Self-organization can be dangerous when it exists without leaders who objectively check and balance how a team is influenced. When order or chaos are disrupted, independent thought within a self-organizing entity will emerge. Some teams may accept this risk as a trade-off for scale and speed. An organization can grow faster and at a lower cost when it self-organizes. However, these teams also then need to accept the risk that certain chaos will exist around how such a team functions at various points in its lifecycle.

Organic adaptation or evolution of any entity has its trade-offs. There will be winners and losers. There will be points of inefficiency or lower than optimal quality. The organization may have moments where it gravitates toward one extreme or another as it learns and evolves. Not every self-organizing entity will survive this sort of battle of the fittest.

A future where self-organization is more and more prevalent is not a dark future at all. The benefits indeed outweigh the risks. Self-organization is an excellent tool for the disruptive leader. It requires teams that are made up of people who value and understand accountability. It assumes, then, that these self-reliant individuals have found their way. They know who they are and the role they must support to help make the team successful. The disruptive leader helps members of the team discover themselves. A self-organized team can only find success when each person knows their role, the roles that depend on them, their strengths, and their individual limitations.

Strong leaders recognize that they must modify behaviors and influence aspects of the team to keep its growth and scale in check. If not, these leaders recognize and understand the tradeoff they may be making. This simply means that they are accepting potential failure as a strategy in the short term. Sometimes we fail on purpose and recognize that our own self destruction will eventually lead to success down the road.

Self-organization can be a bumpy ride with a steep learning curve for an organization that has traditionally relied on more command and control from its leaders. Organizations must unite teams without formal authority and ignite partnerships to be successful. Accountable leaders recognize that they are not always in control of the situation. In fact, the greatest leaders are often far greater at influencing. These individuals know what it takes to lead without specific or defined authority to do so. These leaders know what strings to pull and buttons to push to ensure that the team is capable of rallying toward a common goal.

My dad had 5 rules he would recite to my brothers and I when we were kids. The rules included "Be honest, do the right thing, do your best, finish what you start, and take care of family in good times and bad". Disruptive leadership reflects most of these principles in one way or another. Honesty and transparency create trust. Doing the right thing is not only bold but it also requires one to understand what the right thing is. Finishing what you start takes courage and, in the end, only a trusted advisor can be there for those they care about.

When my daughter was born, my dad gave her a book with a hand-written inscription on the back cover. In the note, he told her to find her own song to dance to. When I read it, it made me stop to think about what I would tell my daughter someday. Would I pass down the rules? Is there a rule that I would add or one I might take away? I realized that I would probably agree with him that she needs to find her own music. In fact, I think she needs to forget the rules, for a second, and go disrupt the world. She needs to understand herself and recognize her true potential.

There are 8 core tenets of disruptive leadership. The philosophy behind each of these principles can serve as a guide for anyone looking to become a more effective and efficient leader. Those who study disruptive leadership should also know that it's possible to misinterpret the intent behind these principles. If taken out of context, any aspect of this philosophy could be used for good and for bad. We all know that disruption has the potential to create chaos. It's always important to remember that the disruptive leader is kind. They are empathetic and merciful. They try to do the right thing but recognize that our universe is fractal. Our actions often have a ripple effect we can't or won't quite understand. Teams will sometimes face incredible odds. They will act with little to no information, but, they will try to do the right thing. These principles will keep them honest and true to the task at hand.

1. Be bold
2. Be informed
3. Shape opportunity
4. Provide guidance
5. Build trust
6. Establish partnership
7. Measure results
8. Inspire courage

First and foremost, one must be bold. Never let the details of a situation or a lack of understanding weigh you down or hold you back. There is always an exception policy. Rules are meant to be broken and have no place in a world where disruption and change is around every corner. Having the confidence to be fearless does require an objective point of view. Leaders back up opinions with an evolving hypothesis. They approach problems with a scientific method but are never afraid to creatively imagine what might be possible. A leader isn't as confident in a plan as they are in knowing that the plan will change. In other words, great leaders always have at least a basic understanding of what is happening, but they are flexible and quick to learn or adapt when things change.

Great leaders are also influencers not dictators. They use information and their own courage to shape opportunities. They facilitate decisive and honest decision making with the utmost resolve yet remain adaptable to an ever-changing environment and its conditions. The intelligent leader is a strong communicator who works from a plan and uses contingency to help guide actions or improve quality. The true test of a leader is their ability to lead peers without the title or authority to do so. The disruptive leader rises to the occasion and can influence the team from any role or position.

Leaders are also trusted advisors. Yet, they surround themselves with strong partners and the right people. They are diplomatic but cautious. They are always measuring, testing, gathering feedback, listening, and focusing the team. They use pageantry to build a culture around them. Discipline or rigor are simply tools that allow the leader's teams to rise-up and scale beyond the day to day. These leaders mature and eventually differentiate the team to expand its reach. Great leaders inspire courage. Their fearlessness is contagious, and, because of that, anything is possible.

Our world is dynamic. Our situation is always evolving. It is only natural that such a dynamic environment would fuel a desire to transform. As we work toward a common goal, our resources are limited, and our capabilities are constrained. Our organizations cycle through moments of consolidation and requests from outside forces to do more with less. However, it's not always the quantity but the quality of our actions that makes or breaks our ability to transform and incubate new ideas.

Doing something new isn't as simple as saying "let's do more". More is not always better. One can't just fill the gaps and hope to get by either. It takes guts, discipline, and careful planning to know where and when to "add to" and when to "take away". Pushing back, negotiating, prioritizing, or advising are soft skills that are in high demand among leaders inside an organization. Today's world is cluttered with organizational debt, broken promises, and over committed plans for the next best thing. The disruptive leader can ask, answer, and facilitate one question well. This leader doesn't ask, "What's next?" or "What didn't we do?". They ask themselves and the team, "What is the right thing to do?"

Quality and quantity are a careful balance. Sometimes, leaders, hyper focused on the quality of an idea, become frozen. These leaders are blinded by quality and lose sight of the conditions that the team faces. Intelligent leaders must learn how to avoid a desire for perfection. By the time a team waits for the ideal conditions to act, it is already too late.

Many ancient philosophers believed that there are only a few basic types of human activity. Our machines and organizational processes reflect the beliefs or philosophies of our ancestors. As time passes, we add to or re-imagine what it takes to be successful. Eventually, our plans, process, or organizational structures are institutionalized. We complicate them to protect or defend our beliefs, assumptions, and attitudes. Our own bias creates more and more layers of complexity around how we work, collaborate, or partner with the world around us.

We often overcomplicate our definition of human activities even though the world around us is quite simple. Teams over engineer what must be done, or they over think how things should be done. The potential options to solve a problem or take advantage of an opportunity are endless. The right method or the right solution isn't always clear cut. Disruptive leaders never allow the team to get hung up on the decision. They let the team navigate the situation and leave little to no room for the arm chair audience to question the team's methods, plans, or actions.

There are so many variables that teams will try to over complicate as they work together. If the team's methods, plans, and solution are reasonable and simple then the disruptive leader supports them. Supporting a reasonable and simple plan is difficult. Everyone on a team wants the opportunity to add value. Team's need to carefully construct their plan so that it doesn't feel as if too many voices are pulling the team in multiple directions.

In the end, leaders and their teams are only ever engaged in three things:

1. Thinking - Seek truth and understanding
2. Making - Produce something that doesn't exist
3. Doing - Enable or maintain something that exists

We "think" because there is a hope and a desire in us to seek truth and understanding about ourselves and the environment we are in. Spectators are thinkers. An audience is always watching and learning. Thinking requires one to be an active listener capable of discovery, learning, and adaptation. It also requires a bit of courage as well. One must fearlessly embrace empathy while also being objective enough to really understand what they are an audience to.

"Making" on the other hand is the act of producing something that doesn't exist. This requires a bit of boldness, courage, and trust to take on the unknown and it typically involves careful planning and measurement. Makers in our modern society fearlessly navigate the unknown. The consequences of progress are not always clear cut. It is easy for outsiders to question motivations, desires, decisions, or goals of the maker before and even after the fact. It takes rigor and focus to stay the course and see the forest through the trees.

"Doing" is the defined action that is taken in pursuit of an existing understanding. Doing, in other words, is the act of maintaining something that already exists. Doing often requires partnerships, planning, and its own forms of measurement, and adaptation. Doing can become repetitive and it is easy for leaders and their teams to feel isolated or abandoned and undervalued. Doing therefore requires its own form of courage often seen as tenacity and optimism.

Great thinkers know how to research to create and test a hypothesis. They also help improve understanding through practice. They stay informed and can articulate the problem, its affect, impact, and success criteria. Yet, these leaders also allow opinions to change and take shape over time.

Doers understand methods, resources, maturity, limitations, and the criteria under which things must exist. Doers standardize, operationalize, and ready teams for success.

Makers on the other hand are great at acting on existing, planned, or missing capabilities to incubate new ideas. They are careful to target their ideas for someone. They ultimately take the time to understand who that "someone" is. Makers also understand what their target audience needs. The maker's ideas target capabilities to support needs at a point in time and place. The maker's goal is to create something that is unlike the things that their audience already has or uses. They also understand dependencies and the needs of others.

Great leaders study and clearly understand each aspect of human activity. These leaders understand that a team must be made up of capable individuals who can think, make, and do.

At the same time, the disruptive leader recognizes that we are all different and capable or adapted to different occupations in different ways. Each team is made up of different skills and experiences. Leaders can't expect or assume that any one individual can get the job done. Our divisions of labor make it possible for us to focus and prioritize what makes sense. It's our collective focus then that limits what it is that a team can deliver at any given time. Therefore, every team may need to import skills from time to time or depend on others when they encounter a problem.

Teams work toward an outcome and that outcome is likely to be consumed, relied on, or used in some way. So, teams must also rely on the feedback of those they serve. However, this doesn't make them slaves or servants. The disruptive leader understands that the team's outcome always has a far greater purpose than for those it may immediately serve. This makes them a servant to none and a partner to all. They must believe that a team's common interest has a larger ripple effect on the world. This allows the disruptive leader to think beyond the short term needs or selfish interests of those who might immediately benefit from a solution or situation.

Even when a leader doesn't fully see the ripple effect or understand what it is, they must push the team forward. Their tenacity, hope, and optimism are what makes them human. Their empathy, kindness, and mercy are what makes them strong leaders. Disruptive leaders understand that their job isn't just to influence individuals or lead a team toward a common goal. They must influence an entire community. In doing so, they must in turn help their community understand and reach its potential.

Get There First

Be Bold

Thinking bold requires one to resist the urge to let rules hold you back. It takes courage to navigate the unknown. Pushing through obscurity requires careful thought around the weight of one's actions and the priority by which things should be done. Keeping things simple helps leaders resist the urge to overcomplicate the work a team faces as it navigates a difficult challenge. It can also help to prevent an over commitment of a team trying to push through the fog of a challenging situation. Teams must resist the urge to wait while they try to determine the utopian solution for every problem. Yet, the leader must be grounded by a forward-thinking vision of what is possible.

The disruptive leader knows that there are no rules. Anarchy wins work and creates opportunity. There are all sorts of constraints we must deal with every day in our lives, however, its one's ability to see past these rules and think objectively that will win the day. Work and opportunity can't be solved by rules alone. If you are focused too much on the rules, you won't see the truth, or you will miss what is possible.

My dad had five rules growing up. I jokingly told my dad one day that I would add a sixth rule for my daughter. The sixth rule is that there are no rules. His reaction was loud and violent as I burst into laughter. He wasn't happy. To this day, he thinks I was joking. Truth is, I was serious. The disruptive leader doesn't let the rules hold them back. They must be ready to leave the flock. Independent thought in the right situation and environment needs to be encouraged and celebrated.

Without independent thought, there would be no room for interpretation. Our society wouldn't need judges or lawyers. Even politicians would serve little use to us. We all know that rules are constantly re-interpreted. Our own constitution is wildly debated year after year as the country evolves and things change. Our local laws adapt to new technologies or social norms. Rules always evolve.

The varied circumstances and conditions of any one given opportunity never produce the same situation twice. Partners, solutions, people, timing, environment, competition, maturity, and budget constraints are variables that influence patterns in the way we work and the outcomes we can achieve. Each situation a team faces is unique and must be solved on its own accord.

Leaders who become competent in their craft must reject an instinct to follow a formula or proven path at every turn. Leaders must instead consider the context of the situation they find themselves in. Contextual influences allow leaders and teams to remain objective and bold regardless of their experiences or the checklist they are expected to follow. The art of knowing when to apply science to a situation and when to rely on faith, instinct, and creativity is a learned skill that takes practice and experience. It is what sets human ingenuity apart from nature.

Our faith in the possible makes us a great creator. It also makes us equally a great destroyer. This dichotomy is one that humanity has wrestled with internally and externally for centuries. The disruptive leader understands and respects this balance. They are bold but cautious in how they introduce new ideas into the world.

Our actions often reflect nature. Yet, we can also imagine things beyond our assumptions about the rules of the natural world. This is what allows us to understand other possibilities. A team at work can shake even the most basic of understandings as it invents. One must take the opportunities they are given and make the best of them to learn how to influence and move tactfully in a given situation. Disruptive leaders will incrementally solve problems testing and learning as they go. However, they may also skip ahead and take a chance on an iteration that perhaps is unproven or not a natural progression for the team.

The natural world evolves by improving an organism through constant testing and learning. In the animal kingdom you will find creatures that slither or evolve limbs to walk and wings to fly. What you won't find is a wheel. The wheel is a simple machine that requires an axle. If evolved, it's initial iteration or state of existence would serve no purpose, therefore, the wheel is highly unlikely to exist in the animal kingdom. Humans though, as thinkers and makers, can conceive of such a machine because our iterations don't always have to reflect the natural world of test, learn, and evolve.

Competent people with perhaps the best of intentions invent formulas for success in the name of getting work done for one reason or another. These well-intentioned individuals can poison the tree. Leaders must reject the temptation to bite into this sort of fruit without examining it first. It is easy to become complacent and repeat an idea or task without first evaluating the conditions. Leaders must coach teams to be vigilant and mindful of repetition or re-use. Individuals must learn to cut to the heart of an ask and recognize unique elements that will influence the relevancy of tasks and objectives in the plan.

Over the years, I have learned this lesson well. At a time when retailers were discovering double digit growth from digital commerce, they were missing the much larger picture of what customers wanted or needed from an online experience. Most of my clients applied the same creative process that had made them successful in the physical store to the web. This meant that true disruption and transformation was slow to progress.

Many retailers created beautiful engaging websites or mobile applications that felt like a shopping experience in the store, but, they failed to solve the barriers to purchase or distribution. Technology changed along the way and this made it easier for all of us to connect experiences at the scale of the web. Retail became less tied to the limited resources within the enterprise, yet, the shopping experience still didn't solve for real customer issues. Feature bloat clouded everyone's judgement for many years. Meanwhile, the mass offer continued to be cheaper than a more contextualized or relevant promotion.

Slowly, retailers shifted from a world of in-store merchandising, weekly circulars, and monthly catalogs to digital experiences. When they did, they also brought the baggage of their old world with them. Executives fought for shelf space and content on the pages of a web experience whether it made sense to a customer or not. We focused on content and analytics to drive conversion. We became so wrapped up in the sale that we forgot about the customer's preferences. Many retailers failed to really understand the power of engagement in most shopping experiences during the early days of digital commerce. They treated the shopping experience like a physical store. Acquisition felt like foot traffic. Executives would even walk the walls of printed layouts the way that teams had done with the weekly circular or other print ads for years. Commerce developers spent the better half of a decade coding the complex rules of a physical catalog or point of sale system. They migrated a hundred years of retail baggage online in the name of digital commerce.

The web was not a physical store. Yet, it was easier to treat it like one and it made sense to people when we did. For the most part, this likely helped customers adopt internet shopping faster. If it felt right to the business, it probably felt more familiar to customers as well. This, in turn, helped to make the transition from physical to digital more acceptable. Retailers re-used their business processes and the lessons they had learned over the decades from a physical world. Teams simply applied them to a new digital one. In the end, organizations were left with debt. Lots and lots of technical debt that made releases slow and aggravating. It would take the next decade to transform and shift the mindset of early digital commerce. A convergence of new or emerging technologies that impacted customer experiences also helped technologists and marketers re-imagine what was possible.

As the world evolved, business users began to take on more responsibility and control over the user experience. Things became faster and more adaptable, but, most retailers continued to apply the same old formulas for success offline to a digital world. Many retailers were slow to see the forest through the trees. Their lack of objective thought around why the web was different left them with a beautiful design that no one shopped. Meanwhile, they missed an opportunity to fulfill faster and engage more.

In the end, most digital commerce experiences, for many years, lacked a flexible foundation that could solve new challenges or tackle larger issues. The piles of debt they took on to launch and maintain weighed them down and held them back.

My clients who embraced a much bolder perspective won the day. This meant that they often took the time to test the unknown or identify barriers and waste in a system that digital could overcome. User experience in this way was not just about what the customer wanted but about what the customer didn't know they needed. This approach isn't easy, and it requires a keen eye for solving the right problem at the right time. It also requires quite a bit of flexibility to change the plan while sticking to the core beliefs or values that are the underpinning of an initiative.

A team's course of action should be based on a foundational

strategy that exists to solve problems of all types within the context of any given situation. Training leaders to solve problems like this takes time and so it's not something one can hope to implement in an organization or on a team overnight. Leaders must condition themselves to focus on a single question while having an open mind to any possible solution.

No matter how crazy an idea is, history will judge you on results. Be bold and decisive in your actions and seek out opportunities that will ultimately yield the greatest results.

We all look out ahead when we plan. We set goals that are based on a strategy and we work backward to define next steps. We baseline our projection as a pile of things that we believe are most likely to happen. In other words, we create a plan that we believe is achievable. We base our forecast or prediction about the future on knowledge of what was successful or acceptable in the past. We take the lessons that we have learned, and we contextualize them with the potential for risk in the future. We think about the reserve and contingency we might need to achieve our plan and we set the expectation slightly lower than what we know it took to complete the work in the past. Our vision feels like a stretch but it's also comfortably achievable. It fits neatly into the construct of our past as a reflection of what we know makes sense. In the end, even when we are successful, this approach will leave a lot on the table. There is a lot more we could have done. The safe and achievable solution is not always a bold one.

A team executes on a plane of time and possibility. The team's past and the lessons they learn along the way will limit their ability to see the future. Poor leaders will try to stay this course and focus solely on a vision that makes sense when compared to the past or lessons the team has learned as it works together. The disruptive leader is bold because they objectively see beyond what is likely or conceivable.

These leaders see what's truly possible. They understand that a team's true potential has little to do with what is likely to happen. They also see little need to create a stretch objective for the team without first considering a more ideal end state. These leaders look for alternative courses of action or other solutions that could achieve a more ideal outcome. The disruptive leader is adept at re-imagining a team's potential. They see other possibilities and the alternative paths a team could take to achieve them. They can solve a complex problem with a simple solution or make something immature lead them to a more ideal state.

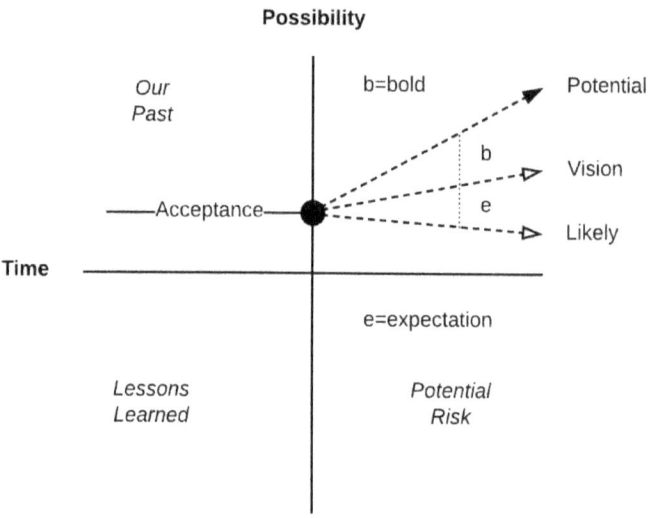

Staying on the path of what is likely to happen is a safe bet to make. When a team's expectations are low, and their vision seems achievable, it is easy for them to accept a safe path as the best solution. The acceptable solution always feels familiar and proven. The team survives by understanding the risk. It is very difficult for them to think beyond what they already know. It is even harder to get an organization to take chances or accept risks that have punished or plagued teams in the past.

Leaders know that people make decisions by using what they know from the past. This is one way that a team keeps itself protected or under committed to the solution. However, the disruptive leader knows that individuals must imagine a world where anything is possible. If this is not a consideration, then they will fail to see an alternative path forward. The disruptive leader temporarily blocks out what they know so that they can be objective. They look for clues in the environment to unlock opportunities that will inspire the team. These leaders are bold and well versed in the art of what is possible.

Any situation has the potential to be exceptional. Bold opportunities are all around us when we look beyond the everyday patterns and formulas of our work. Leaders who are blinded by rules and familiarity will often drive disappointing results. Those who only work from a checklist or a memorized set of standard solutions that they apply to each initiative or assignment walk along a fine line of pending disaster. On the other hand, clear and logical thinking will always prevail. It's much more valuable to surround yourself with those who have an ability to analyze a situation correctly, recognize critical objectives, understand outcomes, and devise a realistic solution.

As we work, confusion and obscurity are commonplace. Sometimes we discover information late in the process. Often, we deal with exaggerated or misleading information. Situations can surprise us, or things can evolve along the way. Change should be expected.

External leaders that influence a team likely do not have clear insight into a given situation. It's fair to assume that these leaders are not acting with malice or lacking intelligence when they miss-direct a team. Instead, they are confused or miss-guided. The disruptive leader doesn't allow the frustrations of external leaders to get the best of the team. A leader's courage to be bold in the face of doubt or failure is critical to a team's success. An external leader's point of view or understanding of what is going on is likely distorted by the way that the team or its larger organization is measuring work or reporting on the outcome of a plan. It is important to remember that teams will behave the way they are measured. The disruptive leader faces this problem head on.

There are many reasons why an external leader may be confused or misguided. One example might be that they are spread thin across the organization and likely aren't paying close attention to the work at its core. This lack of visibility is reason enough that team members themselves need to commit to the details of the planned activities they are executing. External leaders should look to influence instead of control the situation their teams are faced with. Leaders within the team need to facilitate consistent and effective communication to empower and engage external influences. The disruptive leader must remain steadfast in their convictions despite outside influences or irrational requests. Great leaders balance their conviction with an ability to learn and adapt. They also think objectively while taking accountability for the team's failure and success.

Detailed information is often only revealed to us as time passes or work is completed. Information is often not available in the beginning. Information filters up and down an organization or situation like a funnel. The higher up in the funnel a task is defined, the less detail it will have. The closer to the work that an activity is defined, the more narrowed and detailed it will be. There is much more confidence lower in the funnel where detail exists close to the work in progress.

The same principles of clarity or obscurity in the funnel are true for time and space. A task that is executed in real time should have more information and context available than a potential task that the team might take on at a future time. As technology advances and data becomes more readily available, it will be integrated with algorithms that can help predict and inform work. This means that things further out in space and time are far more predictable.

Teams and individuals will have more and more power at their fingertips to make decisions or understand the situation. The disruptive leader helps the team remain vigilant and doesn't let the complacency that can emerge from having predictive data override logical decision making. These leaders understand the importance of weighting criteria before making decisions. They also consider the potential impact of more than one solution.

Leaders must rely on teams within teams. Small groups of individuals must adapt as they work. This means adjusting the plan even when they don't have all the answers, or a clear path identified to move forward. In fact, smaller teams should be able to work with little to no information at all. These teams should learn to take initiative by processing both explicit and implicit information in their environment. Leaders need not worry that the details are undefined and should trust but verify that the team is acting. When a team fails to move forward, leaders must find constructive ways to let teams navigate the unknown.

The disruptive leader establishes various methods for feeding the team with a continuous stream of known work items by partnering with those that can help to funnel the high-level strategy into more defined activities. Rather than dictating tasks to a team, these leaders allow individual team members to determine the best course of action at a working level.

Disruptive leaders also ask the team to work incrementally so that they can learn. The team should measure success based on an individual's ability to operationalize clear intent. The disruptive leader focuses on providing and measuring clear intent as a way of giving a team room to operate. If the team has less constraint around how they solve a problem, they are likely to be more creative or innovative. In other words, a team's ability to follow a detailed plan without ever changing it is not a measure of success.

Great leaders will work hard to keep the team unblocked so that individuals can continuously work without the burden or pressure of too many obstacles. These leaders often accomplish this by creating contingency for various elements of the unknown. Leaders should never try to control too much detail. They provide direction and guard rails while giving teams the freedom to take the right action.

Teams can't allow themselves to become paralyzed or shocked by obscurity. They must "take action" quickly and often. The disruptive leader helps a team move forward even when they do not have enough information or when they are dealing with misguided, non-sensible, and ill-informed directives.

Disruptive leaders learn to turn a failure, into a success, make the abnormal, normal and navigate the uncertain, until it is certain. These leaders empower individuals to overcome hurdles and train them to seek creative ways of ensuring that they do not fall behind.

At the same time, the lack of information a team possesses should serve to energize them. Fear and emotion about the unknown is only natural. Disruptive leaders need to learn to channel this energy in a positive way. An energized team will seek vital information through research, discovery, and collaboration. Rather than operating blindly, leaders should be stimulated in a positive way to test, measure, and learn. A lack of information can create apathy.

Teams can give up or give in when the task at hand feels impossible. Leaders recognize that it is important for individuals to remain confident in what they are doing. Instead of becoming listless when information is scarce, teams and leaders should recognize that a lack of information about their given situation is normal. When obscurity feels normal, it is much easier for a team to rise to the occasion and take quick action to resolve the situation or clear the fog.

The way a larger organization behaves and how it manages its own internal operations dictates how leaders and teams will behave. Individuals can become institutionalized by a larger organization's mandates. This means that they blindly take actions or work hard to defend activities in defense of their own position or stature within the organization. An institutionalized team will protect itself and prevent change or thought leadership that deviates from the normal practices of the broader organization. The disruptive leader sees beyond the policies set up to protect the institution and learns how to influence, change, or use them as an advantage.

Institutionalized teams can sometimes have tunnel vision. This means that they have a lot of information or knowledge about what they are working on but very little information about how it fits into the bigger picture. These types of teams aimlessly complete tasks without any understanding of what is going on within the other groups that may be working around them. An institutionalized team's focus and complacency stems from the compartmentalization of information trapped as value in the larger organization.

Regardless of why the team is indifferent, it is likely that a lack of information will only make morale worse. Individuals that are apathetic or blinded by a lack of information before work begins will then be apathetic to most of the ongoing efforts of the team. They likely won't see or understand the opportunities in hand. This means that an indifferent team likely won't have the motivation to work through a challenge or take advantage of a new opportunity meant to change or improve their situation. Poor leaders will see these teams as ungrateful and they will have a hard time lifting the morale of the organization.

Leaders must find ways to help the team see past what they don't know. Transparency is one tool that a leader has at their disposal to help show the team what is or isn't normal. An open organization has nothing to hide about why a lack of information may exist at any given moment. The disruptive leader will open lines of communication and create more transparency to break down the walls of an organization. This tactic will help the team understand their goals and their role in the broader situation or environment where they are working.

The approach, plan, and the defined work should be simple or to the point. Methodologies that are hard to understand or cumbersome are not likely to be adopted. The same is true for a plan that is long winded and overly complicated. Disruptive leaders know how to use maturity as a guide for defining iteration. These leaders understand that the team needs to crawl before it can run.

Disruptive leaders also work backwards from a vision to ensure that the team has realistic milestones that they can work toward. It's easy for an energetic and optimistic team to over indulge itself in the idea of a utopian state. Daydreaming too much on what the right thing to do "is" can push a team off course. The disruptive leader focuses less on what "could be" under the right conditions and more on what "should be" in the context of the existing situation and maturity of the team.

Complex work can be confusing. It's easy for people to lose

direction while they try to take advantage of an opportunity. Whether integrating and onboarding external teams or encountering unforeseen challenges it's easy for a team to lose sight of their purpose, objectives, or priority.

Leaders must be able to work under duress and within difficult timelines and constraints. The stress of the environment or situation a leader is in should not impact their actions or decisions. Teams must work together to creatively solution and solve problems within the context of a given situation. Leaders must be of good health and mind to facilitate problem solving despite the difficult conditions that the team is in.

Leaders also face the ultimate dilemma. If the work requires an involved effort or complex solution, the risk or potential for things to fail goes up. Yet, a much more simplified effort or lower fidelity solution decreases the chance for failure but may not match the requirements. It is also possible that a simplified version or solution may not achieve the totality of the outcome the team was hoping for. Therefore, simplicity is not a cure for everything but rather a consideration.

Methods, plans, and requirements should not be complicated or elaborate on their own. The audience they are intended for should clearly understand them. It is, however, important to note that these things, in totality, may contain various levels of complexity that apply to different teams or levels of an organization in various ways.

Over the years, I have learned that simplicity is often the hardest thing to influence on a team. There are leaders, in very senior positions, that want to control the outcome and believe that detail is the best way for them to do so. They often jump from strategic to tactical in a single conversation. They fail to understand the true talents around them. They try to plug holes with resources or assets but start with bad assumptions and a misunderstanding of capabilities.

These leaders also have a hard time organizing thoughts at a certain level above the plan. They want commitments made long before the team even understands the goals or intent. They demand results that don't fit the strategy, or, they confuse the situation by communicating with the wrong people at the wrong time.

There is only one way that I have been able to deal with this sort of chaos. I have been consistent in my message. I refuse to accept certain behaviors or allow them to influence the situation. I redirect people to the appropriate channel or level of the conversation.

Navigating an organization with poor leadership isn't easy, and it sometimes can feel like you are saying "no". When done correctly, "no", can feel like, "yes", and people will eventually thank you for keeping them focused. Then again, this sort of maneuver isn't always appreciated or understood. In the most extreme of circumstances, it can be downright impossible.

When all else fails, the Barney Fife method can come in handy. Barney is a fictional character from the Andy Griffith Show which first aired in the 1960s. The character is a deputy sheriff in the sleepy town of Mayberry, North Carolina. He only caries one bullet in his shirt pocket, so, the character must be a bit wily in most situations. In some scenarios, it's a lot easier to walk into a room or engage with a difficult team knowing that you only have one bullet. Plan to use it wisely. Rather than guns blazing, be prepared to duck and cover until you get the perfect opportunity to fire your gun. Sometimes, it only takes one "win" to seize the moment and gain the right momentum to push forward.

Regardless of the strength of leadership at various echelons of the organization, each level of any hierarchy needs to find a way to be in sync with the overall goals and common interest of a team. Methods, plans, and requirements must be relevant and consumable. These artifacts are intended to guide an executional team. Smaller teams execute activities guided by a larger strategy. These goals and objectives can be established or consumed from outside the team to align an organization. They can also help influence and focus the team as they work toward a larger goal.

All teams should decompose work items until they are smaller and more achievable. Work should be decomposed to be measured against the smallest possible building block that is used to track resource or asset allocation. The decomposition of work into small more achievable items needs to be balanced with the idea of keeping the plan simple. It should never over burden the team so that they can't quickly work or communicate.

In this way, the individual should complete work as time progresses and not all at once later in the plan. Poor leaders will allow individuals to carry too much work from increment to increment never completing a task until the end. Teams that work on one activity here and one activity there without ever completing a task are more likely to end up with a bottle neck later in the process.

Work should be completed as the team moves in iteration toward an objective. Even outside of an individual increment of work, larger activities should never complete "all at once" at the end of the plan. If they do, then the team has failed to define work that is actionable within an iteration or a plan.

Plans need to convey only a few things:
1. Overview of the situation
2. Clear intent, objectives, and criteria for success
3. Space/time in which the work is to be completed
4. Resources needed to accomplish the work

5. Methods for collaboration & communication

Leaders facilitate efforts to further deconstruct work into an actionable set of activities and coach the team as they commit to the effort needed to achieve the intent and objectives in the plan. Activities are defined as the prioritized inventory of potential effort related to key objectives. Essentially, future work items become an evolving inventory of what might be "up next" in the plan.

Leaders need to ensure that the team isn't distracted by future action items. Potential downstream work should be defined at a high level until team members are ready to plan and commit to it. Teams should limit or control the size of their inventories to fit within the context of executional time and space.

Work items should be small enough that collaboration is easy. Teams with too many leaders or too many cooks in the kitchen will wrestle with disaster. Successful teams rely on a unified voice to coach them toward success. Resources and the skills found on a team should balance each other out and work in unison. No one voice should over power others so that they can't effectively execute their own role. Poor leaders will burden a team with opinions, distract them, or over load them with unimportant activities so that they can't effectively do their own job within the team.

Disruptive leaders harmonize dependencies on the team so that one group or individual is never working outside of their intended role. These leaders also prevent individual team members or groups from working too far ahead of the others. Work should feel like a game of leap frog. Some members will set up to support or feed the others as they work without getting so far ahead that the trailing effort can't keep up.

Simple plans and instructions should also be timely. By

publishing information quickly and often in a simple format, leaders or team members can convey quick soundbites of direction. These small but efficient and timely notes give individual team members more than enough time to react.

When it comes to work, the simple way is usually the best way. Direct, clear, and concise is usually the most effective way to plan and communicate. Methods that are easy to adopt and flexible enough to adapt to individual situations are best. Change should feel like a normal part of any plan, method, or communication. Leaders who keep their teams un-encumbered by complex and overly engineered process / planning will minimize confusion and increase the chance for success.

Be Informed

Disruptive leaders use timely information to apply the right amount of influence at the right time. It's important for a leader to understand the environment, situation, and conditions. Pursuing that understanding can't slow down the team or hold back decision making. The intelligent leader focuses on just enough information at just the right time.

The disruptive leader ensures that the fidelity and maturity of a team's goals or objective are well understood within the context of a given situation. An individual team should focus on one single primary goal at a time. That goal should have a clearly defined end state that leaders know the team can influence in a measurable way. The work needed to achieve the overall goal should be prioritized and concentrated on the most valuable potential outcome. The outcome or output of a team should have multiple objectives tied to it that the team can deliver on incrementally.

A majority of the team's effort should be applied to the highest priority activities. Leaders need to ensure that scale is achieved and applied before a team executes lower priority tasks and objectives. To balance the plan, a leader can negotiate a much lower fidelity or a less mature end state for less valuable activities.

Our healthcare system went through quite a bit of change as we entered the digital age. It goes without saying that the human experiment to institutionalize healthcare isn't that old in the first place. Much of the science has been around for less than a few centuries. Even our understanding and industrialization of modern medicine has only evolved over a short period of time.

My healthcare clients struggled a great deal with a new regulatory climate that demanded lower cost, less returning visits, and more interoperability to benefit population health. Together, we have worked hard to prioritize a wide variety of competing interests. It hasn't been easy. The public sector and the academic world both keep a tight grasp on our healthcare institution. Beliefs, values, and assumptions are deeply rooted in a hierarchy that is meant to protect the patient from undesirable outcomes. Thinking outside the box in such an environment often requires a totally new construct. There is a lot of weight and emotion tied to existing paradigms. This can make it difficult to re-imagine or change things for the better.

To prioritize cost consolidation and business outcomes together, we have had to identify a new way of measuring, planning, and working. This sort of strategy requires thinking that feels different and abstracted from the defensive layer that governs the existing system.

As healthcare is transformed, hospital systems have spent enormous amounts of money on electronic healthcare systems. They have re-imagined a world that was once institutionalized and in-efficient. A world where data wasn't shared, and systems could not work together. This required them to re-skill and re-organize around new value streams.

What began as a focus on patient experience, health, and safety quickly evolved. Health care providers have realized that patient expectations around technology and experience mirror that of consumers. They are now researching and adapting to a new dynamic in which the consumer's expectations will govern how healthcare is perceived and used by future generations.

Teams must continuously research and discover new opportunities that will allow them to identify priorities, shift focus, or influence a situation. Typically, the greatest opportunity lies where a client or an industry least expects it to. Often, where no one else is focused, there is usually weakness. Leaders find opportunities like this on the fringes of their value chain.

Budget, timing, and resources should correspond with the selection of a primary objective and focal point. Disruptive leaders never default to an equal weighted distribution or allocation of the plan unless it makes sense. These leaders apply the most resources, budget, and time to the primary focus or objective. High value or high impact goals should be used to establish momentum.

Once work begins, a team needs leaders who can advise and unblock the team. In turn, resources need to have self-accountability and self-organization. Teams shouldn't drag leaders down with detail. A leader needs freedom of action to deal with incidents as they occur. Supporting roles within the team should concentrate on helping those producing output. Support roles can't forget that they are there for one reason and that is to make sure an individual contributor who is "making" or "doing" can do their job unobstructed.

Small teams shouldn't look too far into the future. Their work should be simple, clear, and well understood. During a work cycle, teams should focus on the work at hand that they have committed to. Teams working in small cycles must not be disrupted by change. New decisions, based on an evolving or added situation should be made later in the process.

In the absence of information, let a basic framework and an overall objective guide the way. Having these things established, understood, and well adopted will ensure that when the time comes, a team will, without question default to the framework and goals without becoming lost or aimless.

Inevitably teams may find themselves committed to the

impossible. It's likely that a leader will have certain misconceptions or even little to no information as to what assumptions and context lead to the current situation. Priorities are best written in the moment. That means, if a team is focused on the work cycle ahead, establish new priorities and continue to re-evaluate and cleanse activities as the work is completed.

What's possible is best determined by those committing to work at the time that a small and short iteration is starting. There is no use dwelling on bad luck or ill-fated circumstance. Instead, work to understand the current conditions and dependencies the team is facing and find a way to use them as an advantage. Focus on what's possible and move forward in the moment. Leaders who don't clearly understand any of this are usually set to fail.

The brilliant leader knows how to use existing conditions to his or her advantage. Navigating the situation and the environment is key. The disruptive leader studies the environment and uses it as a guide to determine the best course of action. There may be no apparent red flags, yet, understanding conditions of operability or the environment in which they exist, may suddenly give up information about dependencies, gaps, roadblocks, or other pitfalls that might make certain courses of action impossible or illogical.

A team can't always choose the situation or environmental conditions it is faced with. Often, the smaller the team, the less likely it is that it might impact maturity, organizational decision making, or even situational conditions that exist at a given moment. So, disruptive leaders must ensure that decisions make best use of the existing environment or other elements of the situation that can be influenced.

Environment and situation should be an open book. Teams must read the context around them carefully before making any decision related to the design or implementation of a solution that solves the challenge they are facing. For example, if something in the environment is a known risk and likely unstable, it might make sense to protect the team from the risk or recognize the danger with a plan as work progresses. On the other hand, ignoring or hiding the problem is not an effective shield for risks and issues that a team is facing. Disruptive leaders recognize that transparency increases trust. This is critical for a team that needs to feel confident and protected from a problem.

The path toward disruption is a continuous chain or loop in the shape of a helix. Disruption is three dimensional. It has length, breadth, and depth as it cuts through time and space. Our teams are dependent on others. Our strategies are both limited and fueled by the conditions within an environment. So, leaders must work hard to strike a balance between exploiting the team's capabilities and focusing on the dependencies that will make them successful.

Disruptive leaders are constantly thinking in every direction. They are fierce warriors who see the world as multi-dimensional. The path of a disruptive leader is continuously influenced by the "Paladin Helix". The helix derives its name from 7 connected variables within a chain of events. The connections within a helix loop include partnership, acceleration, listening, action, dependency, influence, and need. Each activity represents an implicit or explicit connection that exists between outcome, situation, environment, observation, and strategy.

On one side of the helix, there is a strategy that is influenced by platform commodity, standardization, or rules that help to accelerate a plan. Leaders orchestrate past and present observation as they make decisions. They listen for events to gain awareness of an environment, situation, and the needs streaming in from the other side of the helix. Leaders also create partnerships to improve quality, efficiency, and scale.

The other side of the helix pairs the strategy with an outcome. The team's output influences both the situation and the environment. This outcome is based on needs that exist within the context of a situation. The outcome of the team's work is impacted by dependencies but connected to the strategy through the team's action and its measurement.

Paladin Helix

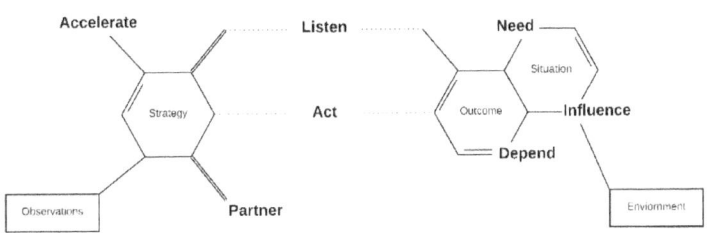

The Paladin Helix pairs a team's vision with its reality. It contains fundamental characteristics which make up the qualities of our work. It is a self-replicating chain of information that connects a plan to a relevant output. Past and present observation come together with analytics, testing, reporting, and other listening capabilities to guide the team's strategic direction. Disruptive leaders understand the importance of momentum and so they partner and accelerate the plan by using contingency, standards, and other efficiencies.

The helix represents a holistic view of work orchestration across the entire spectrum of actuating an outcome. Understanding the continuous nature of discovery in this pattern is one of the most difficult aspects of information gathering. For teams, learning and discovery never end. Disruptive leaders understand that it isn't enough for a team to be informed or to have a great idea at the start of an effort. They must have an understanding that continuously considers all the conditions, tasks, and standards necessary to enable or achieve their goals.

The Paladin Helix represents a constant three-dimensional loop of disruption inside of an organization. When viewed two dimensionally, the helix can help leaders plan for and manage disruption in and around their teams. An organization's helix consists of three main parts

- Assets – Accelerators, partners, dependencies, influence
- Knowledge – Observation & environment
- Capabilities – Listen, strategy, act, outcome, situation

Assets and knowledge are the tangible aspects that feed a self-organizing entity. Capabilities provide the combustion needed to transform assets and knowledge into a disrupting force.

Organizations must rely on assets. They create various accelerators to help jump start projects faster or to run them more efficiently than their competitors. They establish partnership agreements prior to taking on work because they know what gaps need filled. They are always aware of what their teams are good at and what they are not good at. To that end, they never work alone and recognize that all work has its dependencies. They plan for and count on others to deliver with them. They also recognize that the scope and scale of their influence establishes trust and it inspires others. For that reason, they strive to be thought leaders.

Organizations built with the helix in mind also rely on knowledge gained from experiences past and present. They aggregate observation and store that data for re-use later. They process what they have learned to compare and predict the current and future environment. They build up capabilities that are relevant to their situation and focus in on the outcomes or goals they are hoping to achieve together. Everything they do is guided by strategy. They are stewards of time, money, and resources. They listen, and they act based on the tasks, conditions, and standards in their plans.

Disruptive leaders evaluate and improve their organization's assets, knowledge, and capabilities. They take full advantage of the resources at their disposal and fight for what they need to realistically accomplish the task at hand.

When I began working in the telecommunications industry, I brought with me a lot of lessons learned from retail. There was a period where I had implemented the same types of platforms or software solutions for half a dozen clients over a five-year span. Many of these projects looked or seemed identical from a skill or feature set, but, on the inside, they varied in size and complexity tremendously. Some of these programs were a few months and others were a few years. Overall, the use cases were often identical, but the customizations, integrations, and software stack were different.

The helix was a critical part of how I survived each of those implementations. Over time, I developed several ways to accelerate various aspects of the team's progress, but, I had to treat each client differently. Each situation had its own unique challenges or goals that needed to be considered. The partners, political climate, and environment were different but often the dependencies and needs were similar.

By the time I reached one of the larger telecommunications clients in the list of implementations, I had already perfected the art of listening, strategizing, and acting to accomplish various goals and outcomes. I could have never predicted the environment though. We were dependent on an outside vendor who was delayed because of a complex corporate fraud that had taken place in which several inside players had managed to divert IT dollars to a firm they owned. They had hoped to fake what they thought was an easy integration, but their plan collapsed when the work turned out to be harder than they thought.

The entire situation caused the company to re-organize, find new vendors, hire new leaders, and add additional features to mitigate the delay and loss of revenue from the situation. The quality of our work stood on its own and, so, we were then allowed to stay on. Our team helped fight through the disruption and keep things on track while the company re-organized itself. I could have never predicted or planned for such a situation or delay. It was the flexibility of our process and the people on the team that helped us adapt and overcome a difficult time.

If we weren't aligned across both sides of the helix as so many other partners and groups within the company weren't, we could not have survived the delay and subsequent re-imagining of the plan.

A leader will never see everything. The disruptive leader focuses not on what they can't see or what they don't know but on what they can. These leaders use what they do know as a distinct advantage in planning. They read what their own experiences, the situation, and environment are telling them so that they can help the team see the forest through the trees.

As a young man, I attended the Hawk Mountain Search and Rescue school in the Appalachian Mountains of Pennsylvania. There, I became a staff member and a field medic that was assigned to several of the survival school's classes over the years. In early July of 1997, we were hiking along an Appalachian side trail when a call came in over the radio. Lightning had struck up near the fire tower. It had been raining most of the morning and all of us were soaked to the bone. It was really the last thing we had expected to hear that morning.

Several of us raced to the scene. We jogged a long mile up a wet and rocky landscape to reach one of several victims. Five people were injured but the first one we found was the most severely hurt. He had been struck twice. I sent a few of the others with me ahead to help those less injured as I triaged the victim we found along the trail. We treated him for shock and mitigated any burns we could find. We then fashioned a stretcher out of a raincoat and a couple of branches so that we could get him to a landing zone. The Appalachian trail has several landing zones for getting helicopters in and out of remote areas.

After requesting help, we rushed him down off the mountain to the landing zone. The helicopter was there when we arrived. We were also greeted by various other hikers who had heard the call and came to our aid with additional support and medical supplies.

Overall, this is a great example of the helix at play. A team in need, relied on its partners to support it on the mountain. Using radios, it was able to connect to others and communicate effectively. Its partners were listening and sprang into action.

Although we lacked adequate resources, we used our knowledge and observations to take full advantage of the environment around us by creating a make shift stretcher. We were also able to treat the wounded and effectively prioritize or triage our efforts to gain maximum effect.

After reaching the wounded, we were able to accelerate the evacuation because a landing zone was already there to aid us. We tended to the needs of the injured and again used our radios to influence others around us to help improve our situation and outcome. By the time we reached the landing zone that momentum had already paid off. We didn't have to direct the helicopter because our dependencies were met by others involved in the rescue.

In the end, we were able to get all injured parties off the mountain. Each one made a full recovery. This is perhaps an extreme case of how the Paladin Helix can be an effective tool for disrupting what could have been a much worse situation. None the less, it is a great example of how even the simplest of scenarios involving the rescue of an injured hiker requires a complex set of orchestration across several different parties involved.

Shape Opportunity

Opportunities are like clay and need to be molded or fine-tuned so that they are advantageous to the team. Any opportunity or situation is always what you make of it. Shaping the opportunity requires a quick reaction time, some contingency, room to navigate the situation, and a framework for handling decisions.

Operating with agility is a skill that not only requires practice but a certain state of mind. Leaders and individuals on the team must be accountable, flexible, adaptable, and highly capable of quickly moving to take advantage of the right things.

Leaders plan for and know when and how to use contingency. They coach their teams through situations and ensure that problems, blockers, or dependencies are easily handled without stressing individuals. Leaders facilitate decisions and ensure that their teams commit to the work. They do this while ensuring that the team feels as if it is free to move or operate without the weight of outside influences holding them back.

Shaping an opportunity with agility does more for the team than just increase its speed and velocity. It also facilitates the collaboration needed to ensure that a team is more capable and prompt in its decision making. Disruptive leaders use clear and concise communication to influence the team. They can anticipate the probable course of action to get ahead of challenges and opportunities to help the team manage their own destiny.

As the team works together to shape the opportunity, they learn to collaborate more efficiently and effectively. Collaboration requires rapid and timely transmission of information. In today's world that means real time communication and reporting. For teams, it means speed from the start built into how they should be operating.

In the cavalry we had a saying, "There are only three things that really matter. The team must be able to shoot, move, and communicate." Our horse or mechanized vehicle moves to keep us nimble, our weapon systems shoot to suppress the enemy so that we can take or hold ground, and our radios communicate allowing us to quickly coordinate at-scale. The tools, methods, and actions related to those three things are the most critical assets at our disposal on the battlefield. Utilizing and maintaining these things keeps a cavalry officer and his or her team members focused in even the most difficult of situations. More importantly, when all three of these elements are working harmoniously, a cavalry team can win the day by quickly adapting and overcoming other challenges they might face.

There is a lot that one can take from this simple lesson, but, perhaps, none is more important than speed. A team that is always attacking the problem, moving, and collaborating is a team that is likely far more effective at taking advantage of an opportunity quickly.

Disruptive leaders can't let a team operating with real time information end up weighted down with indecisiveness or what ifs. Each individual contributor on a team needs to be skilled at acting with a sense of urgency no matter what the conditions or situation is. Collaboration, agility, and real-time information all go hand in hand to ensure that abrupt changes to plan, delays, or confusion have little effect on a team's progress.

It goes without saying that high morale is critical for maintaining these sorts of behaviors. A happy and excited team is much more likely to collaborate, work fast, share information, make decisions with confidence, and adapt as the situation changes. So, in the end the idea of agility implies both rapidity and flexibility.

Technology and automation, even when the process is deficient, can still help a team move faster than a group with less automation of its process. Leaders must take the time to understand tools and technologies that are available to them. They must ensure that the team uses these assets to help automate work or open lines of communication and collaboration on the team.

Rapid, flexible, and consistent execution performs better than pure numbers. More resources can't replace those who get there first or those that are there just in time with just enough complete. The disruptive leader understands how to create momentum and get the job done at the appropriate scale.

There is good momentum and there is bad momentum. Speed also has its tradeoffs. That is another saying we had in the cavalry. Never volunteer to be the first to do anything. The first person through the door, generally gets shot. That is perhaps a bit morbid, but, the truth is, speed and mobility come with a risk. When you are the first to reach a destination, chances are, you will encounter the most resistance. No one has been there to pave a path yet.

The last wagon on the frontier has a trail to follow. The first explorers, however, may not even have a map. They must tread carefully and learn quickly.

Speed and adaptability are things that need to play together. For example, leaders need to quickly and efficiently issue communication. Whereas, contributors on the team need to learn to anticipate the information and act on assumption, intent, etc. without being blocked.

The team needs to remember that some pre-conceived idea of how things will happen is rarely any indicator of how things will happen. This is further reason why swift action needs to continue to be swift and adaptable. The disruptive leader recognizes this and ensures that the tempo of a team stays consistent not just in the first moments of a plan when the team first forms, but, always.

In the end, it is not just about the action of leaders but the action of everyone to act without instruction. Individuals are accountable for their own role and its dependencies. Team members must work to keep themselves unblocked. They can't rely on or blame others for their situation. This is the only way agility works. It requires self-accountability. Teams that are slow to react, awkward and confused in execution, and clumsy in getting work done are not agile.

The disruptive leader coach's teams so that they expect and plan for roadblocks. Teams shouldn't just assume the best. If they do, they will, in the end, be beaten by competitive or environmental forces. These teams will find themselves dragged down by dependencies and unable to gain an advantageous position to change, incubate, or support the situation.

Disruptive leaders ensure that the team has reserves and contingency. Agility requires speed of action, decision, and an ability to anticipate. One also needs to have room to navigate what they didn't plan for or see coming. Contingency will allow for continuous adaptability. Reserves will create safety, security, and space for the team to breathe. Additional space for a team to execute increases creative potential, improves the outcome, and it can spark an element of surprise and delight for those who work with or are supported by the team.

The Zen Master once said, "It looked as if a team was destined to fail, when suddenly, it anticipated left, but then, it abruptly went right to win the day."

It is important to note that teams who act with agility and leaders who are decisive certainly do take on risk. There is a tradeoff of organizational debt that is incurred when agility is used by a team to work. In other words, sometimes a team that is acting quickly may think about, make, or do things that are unusable or throw away in the long run. The disruptive leader understands debt and helps the team monitor it and use it effectively as leverage over the long term. This is again why contingency is important.

Leaders should use reserves and contingency wisely. Collecting contingency during planning or day to day operations is wasteful if not throttled appropriately. Teams may burn their reserves while taking down debt, navigating the unknown, or shifting priorities. Any one of these activities can be taxing or distracting, so, it's important that the team is careful in how it accumulates or spends its reserves.

The disruptive leader advises the team on how best to use its remaining contingency. There are several ways that a team may use its contingency:

- Fill a gap
- Build momentum
- Change direction
- Establish confidence
- Surprise & delight
- Improve or harden an output
- Influence external behaviors

Regardless of size, team structure, or project scope, contingency will allow for a simultaneous shift at a critical moment to move in a direction that was un-expected, at a time that could not be planned, and with a level of effort that could not have been known.

The key in planning contingency is to make it as generic a bucket as possible. Disruptive leaders will often use their contingency to mass superior resources and target a specific problem at a point in time. Subject matter experts can be used instead of regular team resources for example to solve something that the standard team could not do alone. In general, the use of contingency as a momentum builder can also help with morale as well.

When an existing team encounters a blocker or issue, they may get bogged down by it and frustrated. When the leader has the flexibility to call on a specialized resource, group, or capability to re-direct or boost the existing team's effort, the resulting win can have an overall positive effect. Disruptive leaders also use this tactic as a tool for letting a fresh mind tackle a difficult problem in a new way. A new team member, with a different set of skills, can often jump in and look at an existing situation to define a solution that others on the team might not see right away.

When not being used to fill a gap, change direction, or mass efforts, contingency can have shock value. In fact, contingency often works best when it is not well known by outside entities. Otherwise, it is easy, at an executional level to miss-use it, miss-understand it, or lose sight of how to prioritize it. Transparency is important, but, it's also important for the disruptive leader to increase morale and respond quickly and decisively to feedback. Contingency can surprise and delight when used as a reserved element in the plan.

Leaders who under commit and reserve contingency for the team often do so selfishly. These leaders recognize that outside influences may not see the big picture. Executional contingency and a funnel of uncertainty within an organization go hand in hand. The closer to execution an individual is, the less reserves they will likely need because the team knows more about the work that is going to be executed. The further up the funnel you go, the more contingency one will find in the plan or strategy.

Sometimes that contingency is simply the words used that will help give the team room to navigate when they learn more. Vague descriptions of a strategy near the top of the funnel leave plenty of room for the team to commit in detail as they work. These factors are true for time as well. The further out in time you look, the more contingency there is at the beginning.

Leaders will often hold resources, time, or materials in reserve to help protect the team as well. There is always a percent of a team's plan that is unknown or undefinable. Some portion of that percentage may include things like inefficiency, risk, defective output, operational debt, potential changes, or even the health and welfare of a team. The disruptive leader knows not to assume that a plan or message from the team has accounted for all potential unknowns. These leaders get that it's also important to work with the team to understand their bias toward the effort. Leaders must coach their teams past poor assumptions or a miss-guided view of the work. Every plan should include reserves as a percentage of the total effort.

Some of the reserve may be planned. For example, a set number of resources could be allocated and committed to the work that exceeds the estimate knowing that there will be risk, defect, or administration that is not accounted for in the plan explicitly. Every aspect of the team's time, resources, and work do not need to be planned. It is possible for a leader to overburden a team with planning. A portion of the team's reserves should be held as contingency to avoid over loading the team with too much detail.

Leaders must ensure that the team is always defining contingency as they plan their work efforts. However, when it comes to reserves, it is never just as simple as a blind allocation or application of a percent of the team's effort. This is because not all things are distributed evenly.

For example, on a team, you may have different skills, inputs, outputs, or workstreams. These considerations along with some of the other vectors of time or organization of work could be distributed un-evenly. Over simplifying the use of a "percentage of effort" as an assumption for the reserves that a team needs will likely result in failure when a more detailed plan exists for the work effort.

Intelligent leaders understand how to assess contingency and apply the right amount of reserves. These individuals consider the fact that each unit of effort is not contributing to the same amount of output or type of output. Reserves and contingency must have each contributing factor weighted. For example, it is never; 80% as my plan + 20% as my contingency = 100% of the budget. Instead, the team might have its reserves weighted, 50% as a plan, 10% as collaborative debt, 20% as contingency, 15% as quality remediation, and 5% as risk mitigation = 100% of the budget. A further deconstruction of this sort of planning might weight skill or goals differently as well.

The key point with any elements of reserve that are built into a plan is that most things in life (effort, reward, output) are not distributed evenly. Some inputs that make up a team's contingency contribute more than others. Disruptive leaders must help their teams understand this.

Teams should only simplify or evenly weight the distribution of contingency in plan when it makes sense. There are certainly cases where a leader is painting with a broad brush and evenly weighting an allocation because of the obscurity of the situation and lack of detail in the plan.

External leaders may see the overall reserves of a team or its contingency as a negative strategy when it isn't being used to plan or execute efficiently. Generally, the team might here the term "sandbagging" from leaders who don't quite understand the strategy of holding reserves. This fear could be for good reason. Too much contingency can paralyze a team. As a defensive tactic, additional resources could be hoarded, wasted, or miss-used.

Sometimes external influencers do not recognize or understand the power and pure necessity of contingency either. When this happens, teams may try to mask its existence. A lack of transparency fuels mistrust in the plan. Good leaders know how to spin the team's use of its reserves to influence external stakeholders.

A team's contingency can also be used to influence or change negative behaviors impacting a team. When internal or external forces are acting against the best interest of the team, leaders can use reserves to stay the course. This is often a great strategy for teams or organizations that are maturing or so heavily partnered that they can't quite influence the outcome as much as they would like at certain points in time.

The disruptive leader can maintain effective communication across teams while ensuring that individuals are planning for the unknown or inevitable. These leaders also maintain an understanding of when, how, and why contingency is used. Understanding the use of contingency helps teams educate, establish trust, learn, and grow.

Leaders also factor contingency when defining other expectations about the work. These leaders ensure that the team has room to navigate planning and execution. Contingencies also help shape the opportunity by making it easier to bring new resources, skills, or capabilities to the table.

The reserves a team may need is a factor when defining the makeup and output of the team. Disruptive leaders use contingency to coach teams through challenges related to the fidelity and priority of work. For example, the outcome of thinking, making, or doing something could be standardized or componentized during design to ensure the end state is more extendable. This decision could be made by a team as a contingency even though they have very little information about whether the outcome will need to be adaptable in later iterations of work or once the end state is proven in an operational environment.

Outcome based contingencies are a key reason why surprise and delight may result from the work. The end consumer of an output or the external stakeholders impacted by an outcome of the team will be delighted when the team is able to deliver a more effective or efficient output without impacting expectations that may have been originally established. Competitors can be disrupted, or an environment influenced by contingency in this way as well.

Contingency doesn't always come in handy when there is a problem. It can also be used to exploit an opportunity or react to something outside of the plan that the team has learned as it pushes forward.

On the flip side, momentum and success can also turn into contingency. In other words, teams and leaders should take advantage of unexpected success by asking for additional resources or requesting support when the fire is still hot. When work is completed earlier than expected, a leader can also take advantage of additional room in the plan to exploit known opportunities.

Greater success is rewarded to those who dare to use contingency in new and imaginative ways. These same rewards are rarely gained by those who use contingency only to fight fires and handle the standard day to day issues. The disruptive leader understands that contingency is often the team's most valued commodity.

Leadership decisions are not easy. If every decision you make as a leader seems easy than something you are doing is wrong. Success comes to those who have hard discussions and don't shy away from conflict. More often, than not, the hardest of decisions happen in obscure and uncertain situations. Disruptive leaders take these challenges head on.

The ability to design and define requirements or prioritize the right work for a team to execute is only but the slightest preparation for executing something end to end.

Leaders must know when to act. They also need to know what to do in a specific situation. Those two elements are critical. The "when and how" allows leaders and their teams to act decisively and with confidence. Leaders must also "accept" responsibility. Often, we ask people to "take" responsibility as if there is some option for who should own it. Asking a disruptive leader to "accept" it is a little different. It means that in any defined situation, even if a leader is blind to what is taking place, they must accept that they own some positive action.

Developing these sorts of decision making qualities in leaders is not easy. Academic knowledge is not enough to execute in today's world. Teams need real life examples, case studies, and training that puts them in the situation. More importantly, "at bats" matter. Allowing teams to work on new things will keep them fresh. Inspiration comes from experience. Even more importantly, continuously working off to the side on accelerators, training material, or leaving room for prototypes and proof of concepts to test new theories is also another way to ensure that the right decisions are being made in the moment.

Leaders and their teams must take the initiative. After all, no decision is still a decision to do something. So, even when you feel as if there is not enough information to accept responsibility for acting, a disruptive leader recognizes that they own the outcome and not deciding is ultimately a decision in and of itself. Leaders must accept that they did nothing or too little too late after a given situation occurs.

Decision making should happen regardless of how much information is known. A common rule of thumb is to assume that you only need "just enough". In other words, "just enough information to make a decision" or "just enough requirements and design to start working on a product" or "just enough communication to start". Even when information is vague, the disruptive leader will assemble a team and issue a hasty communication to get them started. In today's world, that communication works best when the team feels like it owns the decision.

Making a team feel like they own the decision starts with making them feel like they own the process and the outcome. Just like the leader, a team that accepts responsibility for the outcome no matter what, is a team that will act with self-accountability. Teams that take pride in and feel like they own both the outcome and the process also have higher morale and will perform with more output.

When a leader is experienced or at least practiced enough to know how and when to act, it will help them deal with and manage change. Unpleasant surprises that occur when a situation is different from what the leader expected will have little effect on their resolve. In fact, even when the situation hardly resembles the plan or assumptions established earlier on, disruptive leaders and teams will navigate flawlessly.

Seasoned leaders that are trained to make decisions and accept responsibility for positive action are far more likely to be successful when the going gets tough. Illogical situations, with an unfavorable environment, and far few resources won't be the problem that a leader focuses on solving. Sometimes, "it is what it is", and a situation just isn't worth fighting. It is far too easy to sit back and criticize the lack of communication at the right time or the confusing instructions provided to the team. Instead, ask, what can the team do with what they have? How do you move forward despite the situation? Again, there is often no sense dwelling in the past other than to note it so that it doesn't happen again.

At the end of the day, one can sit back and criticize just about anything. The same is true with contractual expectations, agreements, and requirements used by a team. When leaders and teams are at a point where they are debating the words in an agreement, communication, plan, or requirements document, then they are likely focused on the wrong thing. It may be too late or too far gone, but, decision making, and collaboration should happen so that the words in a document have far less meaning. The disruptive leader understands that it is almost never worth the time to argue semantics. Words can be debated for thousands of years. Focusing on rigidity of documentation slows teams down, reduces morale, and even reduces the quality of the outcome. Even a poor decision is likely better than no decision when information is lacking.

When judging the decision of a leader or team, the disruptive leader recognizes that negligence and hesitation are far greater faults than an error in choice related to how something was done. When it comes to the timing of a decision, there is no hard and fast rule as to when a decision should be made. It must be early enough for an action to be effective and not too early in that it fails to meet a changing situation. Understanding the operating environment and the dependencies in which a decision is to be made are critical elements.

Teams should never feel as if they need to have a literal

compliance with a decision. When a situation arises in which a collective decision hasn't been made, the team should feel comfortable taking reasonable action as they see fit. Obviously, it is assumed that the team would act in accordance with some overall plan or standards, none the less, they should feel free to act and accept responsibility for their own decisions. In the moment, there is often little time for research, so, do what is possible, make use of what you know, and have confidence that action rather than hesitation is the honorable choice as a disruptive leader.

Provide Guidance

Leaders provide guidance to teams so that they can influence collaboration and unite individuals to work toward a common objective. In the absence of a formal plan, great leaders are highly capable of organizing just enough information to brief the team or specific individuals to help get them started. The ability to provide guidance requires empathy and an understanding of human behaviors. Leaders know how to organize information, present it, and motivate their teams to contribute to both the high-level brief and the detailed plan.

These leaders are also great stewards who can shepherd people and resources efficiently. Teams that define and decompose actions into small increments are more likely to be successful. The activity of thinking, making, and doing should feel like a nested doll. The smallest of increments at the center should be the least obscure and the most defined. The largest of increments of activity should have the most flexibility to adjust fidelity or definition as more is understood or learned.

Leaders coach teams toward defining actions that are measurable and contain clear criteria of acceptance. This means that work is always reasonable, achievable, and relevant. The conditions and standards that govern a situation matter because they are a consideration by which activities are executed.

Leaders also know that all activities should have clear responsibilities. The disruptive leader trusts but verifies. They rely on others but never assume that what they hear communicated is accurate unless proven.

Leaders put quality first. They understand that quality isn't something that happens after the fact. Quality is always a consideration. Disruptive leaders who get that quality is important shift it as far left in planning and execution as they can. These leaders make it a continuous mechanism for ensuring success.

Teams should never drift aimlessly without some formal plan. Leaders must ensure that a team is committed to a plan that is clear and workable under favorable conditions. A leader's job is to help establish clarity by administrating the commitment to a plan and by unblocking the team to create a more favorable situation. It may seem obvious that a plan is needed but it isn't always obvious what the plan should contain in its most basic form. For starters, an understanding of why and purpose are a primary underpinning of avoiding ignorance. This holds true not just of work but when defining objectives too. In other words, the output of a team should not lack purpose and rationale. A leader's plan may and will frequently change but the idea behind it should remain.

Coordinating "the means" by which activities are to be executed is also a critical component to any plan. The team, its make-up, and the dependencies required to work all go into defining commitment. This is again why disruptive leaders are great stewards. They help the team determine how best to use available resources.

Failure can be the result of an inability to take initiative. Sometimes initiating the plan is the hardest thing to do. Waiting for more information can lead to aimless drifting or slower than optimal progress toward an outcome. It can also make it inherently difficult to turn the ship and impact change. Once expectations are established around the demand for a certain level of information, teams then rarely shift gears. They wait for information and then start on work never looking back. Did they have all the facts? Did they have the right goals or plan in place? Without coaching, an established team likely won't revisit these fundamental questions. A group in motion, remains in motion once it finally gets moving on a plan.

It can be hard enough to get the team started though. Sometimes, a leader can freeze up as they wait for direction that never comes. Teams and those that rely on them can aimlessly drift forward frustrated that no one else has taken the initiative needed to get them started on work or planning.

The Initiative

The prospect waited in desperation.

Looking for some innovation.

The team longed to make the plan.

Was waiting too. For whom? a fan.

Plans take time to develop and so leaders must take the initiative to provide early instruction to a team. If the situation indicates that something is to be expected, individuals should take the initiative to start work as soon as possible. Communication and planning is as implicit as it is explicit. For this reason, detailed information is not needed to start preparation.

In fact, the momentum gained by starting early is so critical that it often will make or break the success of a team. By tackling dependencies early, a team can ensure that they remain unblocked or can start on time once the plan is finalized. Coordinating, validating, and provisioning separately from execution will not only create momentum for the team but it will ensure that they are moving in the right direction at the start. Leaders who take the time to validate their hypothesis before starting are rewarded with a more effective and efficient plan. Long term cost can be reduced by establishing quality early and not near the end of an iteration or work cycle.

Finding ways to train or gain experience is another way of improving quality. Take advantage of down time and find ways to fill the gap between work items. Take on things that will improve morale and build culture. These things may not require a formal plan, but they do need to be identified. Teams that use their time effectively start and finish on time as well. Be efficient not only when you are doing something but also when you are not doing something.

An effective plan also requires a clear understanding of priority. This means that the team should define the order in which activities are to be executed or completed. Priority is based on assumptions, risks, issues, and dependencies that a team or organization is facing. The intelligent leader guides the team through its decision-making process related to priority. These leaders ensure that each factor is carefully considered before deciding what to tackle first, second, or third.

For example; what are the team's assumptions about how the output will evolve or scale over time and why does it do so? or what might be the most complex / highest value item the team could tackle first to learn, build momentum, and potentially reduce risk and dependency long term?

It's also important for a leader to understand external dependencies. Great leaders work to ensure that their team considers the work that needs done by other groups. Disruptive leaders put additional focus on influencing, coordinating, and negotiating plans with external teams who are executing work in the same environment.

Room in the plan for flexibility and change are additional components of a reasonable plan. The disruptive leader helps the team define activities or inventory the work so that there is room to navigate change. They also set expectations within the plan so that the team understands that change is okay. A leader who is capable of changing direction and a team who recognizes and understands how to change in any given moment are critical. Disruptive leaders know that a plan is a living and breathing element of an executional scenario.

It goes without saying that sometimes a team can overcome a lack of planning through the sheer will and determinization of its individual team members. Other habits such as accountability or courage may make it easier for a team or a small group of individuals without a plan to get by. Obviously, this is not ideal, but, it does sometimes work in certain scenarios for periods of time. Some organizations may even encourage leaders in a high-pressure situation to stretch themselves beyond a reasonable bandwidth and allow teams to operate aimlessly while they chase new opportunities. This sort of behavior should not be confused with what it means for a team to have a good workable plan at any given moment.

Eventually, a team working without a plan will self-destruct or implode. Sadly, leaders and organizations often reward these types of bad behaviors. They measure and reward the will of a team over valuing strategy and planning. These organizations typically value success at any cost over the competency of good leadership.

Usually, in this case. the leader is rewarded for bad behavior because a team limped over the finish line despite its situation. Other examples may include leaders who over complicate plans and burden the team. These types of poor leaders may even get by with encouraging bad behaviors because the team pulls through despite is situation. In either case, poor planning and leadership only continue and becomes systemic within an organization.

Leaders who facilitate plans and teams who work together to commit and execute them are more likely to be successful. A plan influences working conditions and creates a more favorable working environment. Leaders understand that it is their job when facilitating a plan to ensure that they are always creating a more favorable situation. These leaders are empathetic to working conditions and often will refrain from encouraging bad behaviors.

The leader must coordinate the plan internally and help the team collaborate externally as well. The disruptive leader recognizes that efforts of the team should never feel disjointed or disparate. Good planning helps to keep teams within teams aligned to a common thread. Regardless of what is happening outside the team, the leader stays the course and keeps the team focused on its objective. Disruptive leaders work hard to align dependencies and shift or change approach when challenges arise. Sometimes planning and collaborating outside the team can distract from the common goal or objective of a team. Too many factors impacting a team can paralyze planning efforts.

Strong leaders don't allow themselves to be dragged along by the situation. This means that they aren't jumping from fire to fire. The disruptive leader rises above every day issues to push a team out beyond what they can see directly in front of them. These leaders improve planning and reset the team's commitment so that individuals can stay out ahead of what is next.

In the fast-paced world of travel, tourism, or logistics my clients have often struggled to rise from the day to day fires they are fighting. Often, these organizations are operating at global scale 24 hours a day and 7 days a week. They are the concierge for their customers who depend on them both in times of leisure and in times of business. One mistake can have a ripple effect in which a vast number of customers lose confidence in a client.

I know this world all too well. Not just because I have spent so many years in the services industry as a consultant, but, because

I grew up in the Great Lakes. I was exposed every summer to the long hours and fast paced tempo of an environment where there are more registered boats than people. I know what it's like to have people depending on you for service. Many of these people have a lot of choices on where they can go and what they might do but very little time to do it in. When they put their confidence in you, it means something. That said, it's hard not to jump when they say jump. We would always say that, "the customer is always right." Then again, my favorite clarifier to that was, "The customer is always right, unless they are stupid."

My travel and tourism clients face quite a few challenges serving customers around the clock. Often, they become so focused on the day to day that they can't think out ahead of where they are in a given moment. We had to re-imagine their partnerships and process to force this sort of thinking into the value stream. We introduced new skills that could provide strategic insights and look at the work in progress more objectively. Together, all of us looked at the inventory of priorities closer and made much more difficult decisions. It required us to think hard about the reserves. It also meant that we really needed to understand the outcomes we were trying to achieve. All of this eventually allowed us to pull each manager out of the day to day fires.

Teams don't work to work. The very act of thinking, making, and doing must have a definite end state in mind. We work toward outcomes. The disruptive leader puts the outcome first to help each team member see or understand what is most important to the group. These leaders also keep the needs of those who will consume the outcome in mind.

Plans also contain actions. When we define activities, it's also critical to remember that these actions must line back up to the intent of the plan and fit within the context of the situation.

Activities or actions are funneled. This means that there is a definite structure or framework in which they fit from a high to low level. This structure allows leaders to navigate obscurity and define a flexible plan in a changing environment that is filled with unknowns. It also opens the door for clear communication and collaboration with outside teams and stakeholders. Whether an action falls into the category of thinking, making, or doing, it should have the same structure or framework of high to low level definition.

As an action moves from obscure to known, it becomes more and more clear. This filtering of uncertainty for any task is what helps leaders understand sizing. High level actions can be determined early on and used to plan and provide direction. As more becomes known about these things, they can be decomposed further into more detailed activities. Concepts like a reserve and contingency once again come into play as work in the funnel is defined. Anything defined, planned or committed at the top of the funnel early on is far larger in size and contains far more contingency and room to navigate the unknown. The activities get smaller the further along and the further into the funnel a filtered activity is.

When planning, it is important to understand where a defined action fits within the framework. Is it a high-level item or something that has been decomposed and validated in a more detailed plan for example? Its size, definition, and goals will generally stay the same assuming the outcome or intent of the plan do not change. However, the actions required to complete will grow as more and more are known about it and decomposed from the parent action.

One of the most important factors in defining action is clarity and timeliness. In fact, it is far more important to keep things clear and prompt than it is to ensure they are in the correct form. This means that a team may sacrifice detail to communicate or start work quickly.

Activities are often much more generalized when factors like obscurity, lack of experience, and a lack of time come into play within the plan. In fact, when time is short, and change is likely, details are unnecessary. Teams that understand this, are much more successful at navigating pressure or confusion.

Detail becomes important, however, when there is plenty of time, more information about the situation, and the team lacks in experience. In this scenario, leaders may mitigate the risk of an inexperienced team by providing training or detailed instruction. They may also take more time to gather feedback or validate that a solution is acceptable.

Simple instruction can take on many different forms. For example, clarity could mean that specific requirements are not defined in lieu of broader strokes painted about the needs and expected output from a situation. Using existing examples to help explain the ask is another way to ensure there is clarity. Are there accelerators, or working examples? Is there an existing sandbox or demo of the planned efforts? Whitepapers or case studies of related efforts? Or are there artifact and deliverable templates that could be re-used? These, are examples of how a disruptive leader can use previously defined actions to make planning and communication with the team much easier.

Teams will stumble when they have too much to worry about or consider. By not defining work or planning any further into the future than what is needed to understand the situation, a leader can also ensure clarity and reduce confusion. Disruptive leaders plan in detail only so far as the team needs to get started. These leaders ensure that the team is defining just enough activities to learn more and effectively navigate the situation.

Leaders also facilitate scenario planning around various things that could happen to the team. They help teams outline what they might do in various situations. At a high level this is often referred to as risk or issue management. In short though, risk and issue management are nothing more than scenario planning "actions to take" when something happens that impacts the team, situation, or output. This planning should include just enough information about how one scenario would be handled over another. It should also establish a mechanism for communicating various decisions where a set number of options exist to solve certain situations. The disruptive leader is confident that the team can handle any reasonable number of situations that might be encountered along the way.

When a scenario is encountered, leaders and teams must act promptly and react quickly. Bad news is not like a fine wine, it doesn't get better with age. So, whether something is happening, or an opportunity has presented itself, a team must be prompt in defining and executing new actions as the situation unfolds.

Never judge a team or its leadership on what is defined or quantified as an action or requirement in the plan unless a thoughtful examination of time, budget, and resources is considered first. A situation can be complex enough as it is. A leader or team should not be bogged down by debate over some set of rules for defining action that in no way considers the conditions at the time.

Leaders must practice their vocabulary. It is very easy, especially when trying to be short and to the point, to state or define an activity in an obscure or ambiguous way. When this happens, the team may struggle to understand the true meaning behind what the leader intended to communicate.

Even if a word or phrase is likely only to be stretched out of its true meaning in the most extreme of situations, there is always a chance that it might be miss-interpreted somehow in other scenarios as well. Leaders shouldn't take this risk.

Short, un-evaluative, un-ambiguous, simple sentences, and common words go a long way toward making an activity in the plan clear. On the flip side, sometimes, common words in a professional setting that are short and simple get miss-used or come with baggage associated with them. It's also possible that contextual elements like maturity and fidelity could be missing and assumed. In either case, it might make sense to invent another phrase or use a less familiar word. By defining something other than what the audience is expecting, the disruptive leader can carefully disassociate a less than optimal meaning from a situation.

As a leader, it is critical to understand that defined words used to clarify actions need to make sense to the person who needs to execute them. A construct like acceptance criteria, when read and executed by a quality expert, might have a different meaning than when read and used by another role on the team to make or do something. The disruptive leader knows that actions in a plan shouldn't just be clear to the person who wrote them or facilitated them but clear to the team who needs to execute them.

Those who execute action are often only one or two items ahead in thinking, thus, long, highly involved activities or even working cycles in a plan are never advisable. Those who execute are also always in a race against time. It is very important for leaders to understand this and have empathy for the executional side of the team. Long and overly-complex actions multiply the chance for misunderstanding or misinterpretation. They also lead teams down the path of ignoring and tuning out information. External teams and leaders are also more likely to lack an understanding of what a team is doing and how their output might impact them.

Leaders who try to put a magnifying glass on their organization lose site of the big picture. Too much time looking at a problem, cycling on requirements or actions also has the same effect. The desired outcome is lost, or the solution becomes no longer positioned to solve the problem.

Leaders need to shoulder the blame when their teams do not understand the plan and actions they are committing to. There is no doubt that teams should be conditioned to interpret and recognize intent behind how things are defined, however, it's the leader who needs to carefully facilitate the right communication on the team to ensure a clear understanding. The disruptive leader needs to accept that a general rule of thumb should be "if something could be miss-understood, it probably will be."

As any defined action is filtered from a level of uncertainty to certainty, it usually must meet several minimum standards. Typically, the team starts by looking out at the horizon to identify high level goals. They start by asking themselves what exactly they are trying to achieve? Those goals eventually become measurable and achievable as objectives. From there, the team begins to deconstruct the objectives into small and actionable activities.

- **Goals** should be defined early and in collaboration with the team who will execute. Leaders need to ensure that the team has just enough information, just in time to execute.

- **Objectives** should be brief & clear. There should be no confusion by those executing, what is meant by parameters, definition, or intent.

- **Tasks** should include essential information. The definition of a task should outline exactly what the activity is and what elements are needed for its outcome to be acceptable.

Probably one of the biggest things that can be taken for granted by a team is quality. In a situation where time is short and information lacking, quality can feel like something a team will get to when it can.

The opposite should be true. Quality should be something that a leader considers always. Quality is a consideration whether the team is prioritizing a plan, defining acceptance criteria for actions, or executing tasks in the plan. Even the most experienced team needs to ensure that they are not complacent when considering quality or when planning the work and monitoring the outcome.

The requirement for quality is absolute in that no leader or team can execute a plan or previously conceived action without some measure of how it will be accepted as a part of the outcome the team is hoping to achieve. Teams that do not measure or monitor acceptance will eventually fail.

Results are clear and decisive when quality measures are in place. Without quality, even the most highly experienced and skilled of teams will be wholly ineffective.

During certain moments, a leader can choose to sacrifice quality for some other advantage. Though temporary, this decision could be used to manage through a difficult situation such as a team staffing issue or a loss of opportunity that outweighs the sacrifice. However, this sacrifice should only be made if a leader knows that the team can regain quality. In this rare instance, the team must be committed to make strides toward regaining quality as soon as possible.

There are three primary elements impacting quality on a team. Leaders must monitor each of these and work toward helping the team improve them if there is a deficiency. Disruptive leaders are highly capable of knowing how to take advantage of a situation where quality is highly degraded because each of these skills is lacking. No one team is perfect, and leaders must weight how much effort they put into controlling each of these factors. Whether or not they influence them, a strong leader must make the best of what they have.

1. Experience / skill
2. Capacity
3. Morale

There are five ways a leader can promote quality within the team. Each of these factors becomes the measuring stick any good leader can use to assess the health of a team, its work, and the potential it may have at being successful. The disruptive leader uses each of these concepts to improve the overall quality of the work.

- **Measure and validate progress.** Did the team do what it set out to do? Is the outcome tested according to acceptance criteria? Is the plan clear and understandable? Does the plan take situation, obscurity, and other factors into account?

- **Communicate clear, brief, and definitive action.** Is there a structure in place for effective and efficient communication? Can the team collaborate? Is communication happening early and often? Does the leader create an open and transparent environment?

- **Continuously listen, learn, and adapt the plan.** Is the team converging toward a common goal? Has the team taken the time to understand objectives, risks, and dependencies? Is the team considering ideas that diverge from the norm? Do new ideas align with the environment and situation? Is the team free to move and shift its priorities?

- **Organize the team to be effective and efficient.** Has careful consideration taken place to design or enhance the team's makeup, skills, roles, process, capacity, and maturity?

- **Establish a culture and expectations.** Are things predictable, rigorous, or standardized? Does the team meet consistently to discuss the past, present, and future? Does the team review priorities, changes, and lessons it has learned? Are leaders considered trusted advisors? Does the team partner externally?

The disruptive leader focuses the work, the team, its skills, and the way it communicates. Leaders recognize that depth is easier to facilitate than breadth. In other words, a stack of things is much easier to maintain quality control over than a line of things is.

The line, however, creates scale. The stack, on the other hand, gives a team depth. A disruptive leader understands how to create leverage by deploying small teams to attack both depth and breadth as components in a larger environment. These leaders seek to harmonize the team's depth and breadth to keep it effective and efficient.

New technologies allow us to automate and matrix our depth and breadth. Teams no longer rely on their own stack. They can simultaneously tap into an infinite array of other capabilities to scale or go deeper in near real time. In a world where a leader has less control or influence over "the line" or "the stack", they must embrace the chaos and ride its wave. Redundancy and the compartmentalization of outages reduces risk. Disruptive leaders take advantage of lower cost scale where depth and breadth are shared or transacted simultaneously. Teams that operate in an on-demand economy must focus on security and protection from issues that can quickly spread like a virus across an organization.

It is also difficult for any one person to maintain quality when working on smaller iterations with goals and objectives that are early and often. Leaders must rely on the entire team for quality and control. They can't allow themselves to be bogged down with the details of a specific iteration or the actions of a small team.

In fact, a leader is best suited to be out in front of any given situation as much as possible. Being in front, lets a leader focus on what is most important to the team. The disruptive leader puts a majority of their effort into ensuring that the highest value and highest risk item is delivered. They also get out in front of challenges the team is facing while ensuring that new opportunities can be exploited.

These leaders never take on the world alone. The disruptive leader understands the need for additional team members to learn, grow, and take accountability. They see this as leverage and so they embrace other team members who step up to lead on the team.

Any lack in quality will exponentially reduce the effectiveness of the team. In the moment, the size and scale of a situation can make quality daunting. Leaders must ensure that the team is confident that they can sustain quality for both the work completed and the work ahead. Goals, objectives, and tasks must be realistic and achievable. Quality must be a consideration in the plan and the team must know that quality is a priority from the very beginning.

Build Trust

When a team establishes expectations and makes commitments it is the leader who enforces these things. Communication is a critical tool that a leader can utilize to consistently bring a team together. Open and consistent communication will keep a team honest, transparent, and committed to its goals. The methods and channels a team uses to communicate depend on the situation that individuals are facing in their role on the team. Strong leaders coach their teams and use strengths, weaknesses, and plans to their advantage to ensure that the team is successful. A great coach will keep the team motivated and free to operate without roadblocks. This isn't an easy task and so leaders must also advise internally and externally to help align everyone that is impacted by the situation or goals of the team.

Agility is important for the team. It is also important for leaders. Those who coach, facilitate, and manage a situation must be just as flexible as the team. This means that leaders should work as closely as they can with those they directly communicate with. Communication itself should be fast and reliable.

What does close really mean? In today's world, that may not mean that a leader needs to have a physical presence; however, it does mean then that they are actively monitoring and engaged in communication and collaboration tools used to supplement or mitigate the challenges of a modern workforce.

Leaders should have empathy for the conditions that the team is facing. They should have a clear view of the environment in which their teams work in. Leaders should create trust but always validate and prove what is true. Physical presence or engagement with the team shouldn't feel overbearing. Leaders need to believe in self-organization but at the same time help to enforce the rules a team has committed themselves to.

With that said, a good leader can't over commit themselves to a single remote location or an external project that takes too much time away from their ability to coach the teams. Even when communication is working well, leaders can't assume that intimate contact with a team isn't important. When things are going well, leaders need to continue to monitor a situation and engage the team using collaboration and reporting tools to maintain situational awareness of plans, dependencies, changes, actions, outcomes, and quality. This will allow them to jump in and help the team at a moment's notice. Communication tools play a critical role in helping leaders coach and facilitate the team through good times and bad.

When a means of communication fails, a leader must still exercise influence over the events. At the end of the day, leadership itself is simply the art of influencing those around you to collectively accomplish some common goal. Leaders who communicate often and reliably are much more likely to be a trusted conduit of information for the team. Trust allows the disruptive leader to exercise more influence.

Sometimes a team can obsess over policy and procedure related to communication. The need to communicate effectively should not result in formalities that prevent a leader or team from releasing information in a timely manner. It should not prevent the leader from working closely with a team or its partners either.

Overbearing procedure or policy can impact the team in several other ways as well. Leaders who take on too much administration without delegation will find themselves failing to be available when the team needs them most. A distracted leader focused on an overly complex process or the desire to spend too much time mulling over requirements and planning documents will ultimately fail to be available to the team when they need them most.

Failure of process, systems, or artifacts is not an excuse for poor communication. Leaders and teams must communicate regardless of what process, technology, or document is missing. The same is true of a team. Just because a leader failed to produce a document, allow for the use of a collaboration technology, or ensure the right process is in place, team members need to be trained in self-accountability when it comes to communication.

Teams should have backup measures of communication when something fails. Leaders also need to ensure that remote members of the team have access to communication capabilities too. The disruptive leader recognizes that so long as the team can move, type, talk, or blink, there is likely some means for them to stay in communication no matter what.

A strong leader will ensure that the team establishes various open lines of communication. It's important though to keep that communication efficient. It should be short, timely, and clear. The act of communicating should not over burden or confuse the team.

When in doubt, visual communication is a proven way to convey complex information. For one, visuals keep things simple and can quickly convey a lot of information in a short time. This is especially true when visual communication exists within a framework or pattern where previously determined definitions or norms are defined to align with it. In today's world, the use of icons, sketching an idea, or creating a diagram all have a much more powerful effect on a team. Leaders are much more effective when they themselves use visuals or coach a team to do so. The disruptive leader uses visualization to tell a story in a simple, clear, and concise way.

Fast and accurate information allows for more timely and effective decision making. Leaders also need to ensure that the team is consistently communicating their availability to support various activities. Great leaders help the team designate additional support when individuals are indisposed. Timely assistance or backup also requires ongoing reporting of information to shared team members or interdependent teams working on related activities.

The disruptive leader creates or appoints roles that function as a conduit of information helping to interconnect the team. These individuals can support leaders when they are unable to facilitate directly. Supporting roles help to keep information flowing in a timely fashion. These roles are often multi-dimensional and skilled or at least knowledgeable broadly across discipline. An appointed conduit builds bridges inside and outside of the team to keep parts and pieces of a plan intact and glued together.

Without information, teams are aimless and uncoordinated. Too much communication is distracting and cumbersome where as too little sent too late is pointless and ineffective. Leaders must help the team determine how much communication is needed to collaborate effectively. The more untrained a team is then the more hands on facilitation they may require.

Coaching begins with paying attention. In other words, being present. Leaders need to be available for their teams. They must understand not just the context of the situation and threats or opportunities in the environment but the skills and capabilities of the team as well. The intelligent leader works with what they have and partners to get what they don't. Knowing where the gaps are and how much it takes to plug them requires a sharp mind and a good eye for effort. The inexperienced leader can rely on the larger team for help in understanding the scope of a situation. Even when the answer is clear, the disruptive leader always coaches the team to help play a role in shaping a plan for a given situation.

Great leaders know how to estimate a situation. They also understand how to define activities and craft plans. The true test though of any leader is their ability to facilitate decision making and action. Without decision and action, even the most perfect of plans will fail. On the other hand, poor plans, when carried out decisively and with enthusiasm may also succeed. So, quite often it isn't the possibility of a plan working as much as it is the confidence a team or organization has in the plan.

Effective leaders guide teams toward execution. Not rigorously staying engaged is exactly where so many leaders go wrong. Brilliant plans fail when a leader doesn't see a plan through to its execution. A leader that assumes that all responsibility and obligation shift toward a self-organizing team once actions are defined and plans committed will fail to understand that even the most experienced team needs ongoing coaching to be successful. Less experienced teams require even more facilitation and attention. However, a leader must never compromise or get in the way of initiative. Good leaders understand that they alone carry the weight and accountability of seeing action through to its outcome.

A disruptive leader knows the strengths and limitations of each team member and uses these as an advantage. These individuals can't be everywhere at once, but, a strong leader knows when to be present and weigh in at the right moments when the team needs them most.

Years ago, I took over work involving some very complex custom applications. There were multiple projects that were all rolling up to a single program taking place. Each was at a different point in their lifecycle and some were yet to launch into the market. Prior to my arrival, things were not going as expected. Information was not being communicated transparently. Expectations around what was possible and when it could be achieved were not set. There were no short-term goals, and, worse yet, the team was spinning on several blocking issues.

Despite these challenges, there was reluctance to change. For starters, morale was low because the team had been working weekend after weekend in the name of getting the project done. There were photos of several martyrs already on the walls and more team members were standing in line ready to sacrifice themselves for the good of the team.

As complex as the work was, one thing was certain, communication needed to change first. For starters, the team needed some achievable wins, so, goals were reset to be more incremental. Secondly, the team needed to be open and transparent about where they were. So, work was not only re-organized, but, made available for everyone to see. People were given a break and more communication around prioritization and fidelity was put in place.

A funny thing started to happen. The team cleansed itself of some of the bad eggs. People with the wrong lens and a lack of objective thought left. Others embraced a new way of working. Our open and transparent working environment made it easier to demo progress. We also made sure that work was defined in a way that it could be incrementally completed. Prior to the changes, the team had been executing like a hockey stick. This means, they were carrying work over from one cycle to the next, with the goal of completing everything all at once toward the end of the project. With a more executable plan, velocity and output also started to improve. Quality went up and the team began to see more thought leadership as well.

However, none of these changes would have lasted without another important shift. One that could have easily been over looked. It was a systemic contributor to the problem. The remaining people on the team needed to take on new roles and responsibilities. Not everyone, per say, but, many of the people whose thoughts lacked objectivity, did need to shift their roles. Putting people in the right roles at the right time was a key factor for improving the work. Pairing up those who could help each other and taking the time to understand everyone's talents helped the team re-organize and re-skill much faster.

As a leader, I couldn't change all things at once. I had to slowly make behavior changes by measuring the teams differently than they had been. Process and people improvements followed a re-imagining of how we were using technology to govern and solve our challenges. Each step of the way, I had to physically examine and review progress. That meant demos of work completed, reviews of the plan, and inspection of skills or capabilities.

Leaders can't simply rely on communication from the team as a validation of what outcomes have been achieved. They need to actively review action and enforce the ground rules a team has agreed to. Furthermore, leaders should never just rely on reports about what has been completed or achieved. They should review progress and demo working products or services.

It isn't always practical to change resources when a team becomes unreliable and so a good leader knows how to use more intimate coaching of team members when discipline or morale are low. Paying attention allows leaders to monitor risks and dependencies while facilitating the team's ability to react and adapt. Change isn't easy, and it really does require a strong leader to help a team navigate it. This is especially true when a team is navigating the unknown and trying to focus clearly on a single task.

Coaches demand efficiency and challenge teams to mature their capabilities and process. By facilitating retrospectives, securing adequate resources, and ensuring that adaptation is a part of ongoing planning or commitment, a strong leader can evolve the team and maximize its output.

Leaders also monitor plans and actions to ensure that team members are not executing unwarranted activities. Unnecessary meetings, over communication, supporting unprioritized product components or services are just a few of the ways a team can lose focus and work activities that go above and beyond what is needed to get the job done.

Leaders look to mitigate the impact of inactivity or indifference on the team. They influence behaviors and coach teams toward understanding intent. They also inspire individuals to take the initiative and own their own destiny. Teams must detect errors in the work or issues early and fix them quickly. The leader's job is to enforce this and delegate to those on the team who will champion it.

Leaders know that at some point defined activities will be miss-understood. They also recognize that team members will likely talk past each other. The disruptive leader carefully considers the experiences, motives, or incentives of each person on the team. They help the team craft messages that will gain trust and adoption. Requirements, visualization, plans, or simple verbal instructions can be miss-interpreted. Everyone perceives information in a different way. We have all played the childhood game of telephone and know that communication that is passed along or shared between teams is likely to change as it passes from person to person.

When people miss-understand they are more likely to take the wrong action or worse yet not take any action at all. Even good intentions can fall flat when they don't line up with the intent of what a leader or team member was trying to communicate. Careful review of action is important. Leaders need to provide quick feedback when they see that something is not well understood. A great coach also validates output by physically reviewing what a team produces. Simple and realistic plans are an easy way to make sure team members are in sync. Leaders also need to clearly define actions and acceptance criteria.

A strategy can be a leader's most valuable resource. It is like a compass that provides direction for the team. Leaders must be capable of strategic thinking. The team needs to be fed with prioritized work via a defined stream of activities. Strategic thinking allows teams to find a common objective, break down the work, and determine priority.

Individuals should have a distinct appreciation for both the work and the capabilities of their team. Great leaders harness their own empathy and compassion to create an accurate mental forecast or model of potential output. These leaders start with clear context for each goal or objective. Personal affinity for both the team and its cause ensures that individuals or external leaders are not over committing teams to the work. None of this is easy or natural for most people. Individual team members can't be expected to monitor the big picture on their own. Leaders facilitate timely communication around contingency, dependency, workload, and resource capacity to establish trust across the team. This open stream of information also lets them keep a more objective eye on areas at risk for miss-communication

Strong leaders are trusted advisors. These leaders not only understand the work, but they also understand the team and its capabilities, skills, or limits. The disruptive leader knows how to monitor a team's pulse and use it to forecast likely outcomes before they happen. Like a sixth sense, the leader knows what a team will do and works backwards to advise other leaders and coach individuals toward success.

A great strategy will guide a team toward the right place at the right time. By clearly defining the desired outcome and known dependencies, strategic thinking guides a team in the face of obscurity. As a guide, the leader becomes a trusted advisor to the team which helps make them a more effective influencer. As trusted advisors, leaders help to facilitate goals and objectives by supporting the team as they look out ahead at a realistic and achievable end state.

Leaders should be equally adept at breaking down a strategy into tactics and additional way points or milestones to help the team navigate toward their objectives. Sometimes the activities required to achieve a milestone are not always that clear. The strategy, however, can guide a team as it moves from point to point in a plan even though it isn't clear up front how this might happen.

A great strategy can exponentially increase the chance for success when combined with high energy and a determined team. Just enough direction can go a long way for a self-motivated team willing to take initiative to go the extra mile. This also supports the fact that a strong leader should be adept at advising. Leaders should also be strategists so that they can help guide and coach the team even in a scenario where outside or internal strategy is absent from the situation.

Disruptive leaders know all too well that they should never rely too heavily on a strategy. Most strategies serve as a guide to get the team started. These constructs quickly become outdated as the team begins to learn and adapt. Too much implicit reliance on an initial strategy for too long can lead to failure. More importantly, teams can get themselves off track completely if they try to follow a strategy too closely. As an adept advisor, disruptive leaders always take the time to evaluate existing strategic thinking so that they can provide recommendations to the team. These leaders continue to use the situation to adapt and guide the team no matter what the strategy may have assumed.

As the team learns, the core intent behind strategic thinking may never change. However, certain aspects of it may still feel dated or unusable. Therefore, continuous adaptation is critical to a team's success. As the situation evolves, the strategy can feel confusing and miss-guided if the team fails to evolve its interpretation. Teams can run into issues and blockers they didn't see coming. They must shift or mature their thinking if they hope to be successful.

Blind adherence to strategy can stop a team dead in its tracks. It is far too easy to miss-interpret things along the way after a strategy is set. Therefore, advising is not a one-time activity completed at the onset of an iteration or during touch and go planning exercises. Disruptive leaders understand that advising is a continuous activity that they must stick with to coach teams through an evolving situation.

Small steps get the job done and pave the way for bigger picture things. Going small helps teams work more successfully. Small could mean setting more focused goals, running shorter cycles of incremental effort, or making sure that the team is executing much more decomposed activities. Teams too are more successful when they are smaller. There are less risks, communication problems, and it is easier for a team to navigate a strategy when it is organized with more cross functional roles involved in the effort. Compartmentalizing dependencies, breaking down larger groups into smaller working teams, and shielding these teams from cascading issues that can snowball as they spread are all ways to make big things feel smaller.

Creating a plan is one thing. Maintaining it is another. It takes continuous thought and effort to keep a plan executable. This is also true for any strategy. It isn't easy to keep a strategy feeling fresh and relevant. More importantly plans and strategic thinking must feel realistic to a team. Leaders need to ensure that goals are within striking distance. Actions should be within the scope or sphere of influence a team has. Goals that go above and beyond the influence that a team has, without considering scale, maturity, and partnerships, are destined to fail without further refinement and focus.

Disruptive leaders continuously ask themselves the same question over and over, "How can I help coach, advise, and unblock the team to keep them moving in the right direction?"

Teams quickly forget the lessons they gain from retrospective or training without real life examples and more experiences or opportunities to be successful. Leaders need to keep in mind that even a team working on the familiar will gain far more experience and confidence when they are challenged by the obscure.

Establish Partnership

Partnerships and alliances are critical for teams. Cooperation between thinkers, makers, and doers forms the foundation of internal team partnerships. Leaders recognize the power of these relationships within the team. They work hard to inspire collaboration.

I began this book when I considered the rules of my grandfather, but, truth be told, this one I probably owe to my grandmother. She would always say that it's not what you know but who you know. That catch phrase was usually hammered home with a story or two about the Great Depression. A period when no one had work and times were beyond tough. Back then, those that did work, usually did so because of who they knew. It was that simple.

There was a second lesson in that saying. I can remember, as a kid, watching the Oliver North coverage. This is where my memory gets a little foggy. She was probably trying to warn me not to associate myself with bad people. For some reason, I remember her warning coming across more like a Cold War spy novel. "It's not what you know. It's who else knows you know it."

Of course, I don't think she would believe that Oliver North would be breaking bread with my friends, his fellow alum, in the chow hall at our forward operating base decades later. Funny, how the universe works that way. That is perhaps the real lesson. "You never know, who you will know, and how they might be important, so, try not to judge too harshly."

Partnership extends beyond the walls of the team. External partners help to create scale for groups that are missing certain capabilities and depth. Diplomatic relationships with external partners create leverage for the team. These relationships allow the team to focus more on what they do best. External partners also create scale or add depth when a team needs it. Leaders facilitate external partnerships and look out ahead to identify the right players to help improve the situation for their teams.

Good coaches know how to use diplomacy as a tool to inspire and motivate. Disruptive leaders create alliances to mass their team's effort at critical moments in the plan. Diplomatic alliances can create scale at just the right time. This means that the team doesn't have to waste valuable resources on a problem. Diplomacy can replace certain portions or levels of reserve. Rather than holding on to certain skills as a dependency, the team can focus more on what it does best. These teams rely on partnerships to help solve problems with a low frequency or mitigate risks with a lower probability. Diplomacy creates efficiency and reduces waste.

Diplomacy can do a lot more for a team than help enhance its contingency and reserves. Disruptive leaders seek out partnerships that can unlock new opportunities as well. These leaders may also create alliances that solve critical challenges or roadblocks. Diplomacy creates momentum by solving problems that may have been holding back the team. The disruptive leader is never afraid of considering partnerships on the fringe of their value chain. Sometimes the most unexpected of alliances can open doors no one on the team expected.

External and internal partnerships on the team work best, at-scale, when the barriers of forming an alliance are lifted. Disruptive leaders recognize the power of creating an eco-system where partnerships can thrive with little to no effort. By reducing the cost or burden on a team to form an alliance, the disruptive leader can help the team source value from partners at a much lower cost to the team.

A free and open marketplace can come with its own challenges as teams work to protect intellectual capital, defend against competition, and operate independently. This sort of living and breathing cooperation has its winners and losers. It takes time, automation, and governance to overcome the tradeoffs. The drawbacks are a barrier to entry that is more difficult for institutionalized teams but easier for those that are operating at a less mature or smaller scale to begin with. Disruptive leaders recognize these things and remain objective in their approach toward building partnerships both externally and internally.

Leaders inspire those around them to work toward a common goal. Individuals that collaborate on a common objective form the nucleus of a team. By working together, these individuals give rise to the fundamental partnership that must continuously exist for a team to be successful. Working together is what makes a team one unified group with a common goal.

The collaboration between leaders and other thinkers, makers, or doers is the most important partnership within the team structure. Collaboration and action without outcome is indecisive. Teams that work on something but never produce or release any tangible or measurable output are aimless and inefficient. Leaders help to ensure that defined action has an intended outcome. Teams must have planned action and purposeful collaboration to organically work toward an objective.

There are three ways that a leader can ensure that a team is at its best. The disruptive leader understands that these three things mean that partnerships are working.

1. Speed and efficiency
2. Ideation & incubation
3. Hardening

Speed and efficiency will allow a team to reach outcomes at a higher velocity. These teams do this without sacrificing quality. Typically, a high velocity team is more experienced. Usually they have worked together longer too. Higher velocity teams come at a cost, but they are more likely to be successful in the long run on complex tasks.

Disruptive leaders will use teams like this to build momentum or solve difficult high-risk challenges. Ideation and the incubation of new ideas requires cross-functional thinking. Innovation is a clear signal that a team is partnering to think, make, or do in an unexpected way. Leaders must care for what they have. Teams must improve what they think, make, or do. Hardening allows the team to tackle continuous improvement of their existing resources, capabilities, or output. Disruptive leaders use hardening as a tactic for enhancing or improving existing output without deviating from the plan. These leaders ensure that each outcome is sustainable and scalable without sacrificing quality.

Often a situation will prevent a leader from exercising things like ideation, incubation, or hardening. In this case, both speed and operational efficiency always takes the front seat. A team that can work toward ensuring that the highest priority outcomes are achieved as quickly as possible with the least amount of resources will find that its velocity frees up team members to work toward stretch objectives over time. Disruptive leaders focus on velocity as a way of improving partnership and collaboration because they know that this will eventually free up capacity for hardening and incubation in the long run.

Adding more team members or resources will not guarantee more output or higher velocity. Leaders can't solve problems by adding bodies to an operationally inefficient team or to an undisciplined group failing to abide by its strategy or plan. Leaders can't assume that more people on a team will achieve the intended outcome faster. More people will more than likely add to the problem and create more cost and inefficiency for the team.

Every team is going to have a slightly different make up in terms of roles and responsibilities. It is up to a leader to ensure that the capacity of any given team to achieve its planned outcome makes sense given both the team make up and the conditions surrounding the situation. Disruptive leaders rely on the team to make commitments, but they protect an overly optimistic team from setting itself up for failure.

The same outcome could require totally different teams, roles, or even responsibilities if/and when the conditions of each effort are totally different between the two situations. Leaders must learn to coach and advise their teams to understand this concept. All too often, the team will rely too heavily on experience or strategy without considering the nuances of the situation.

It is also important to break up a team into supporting roles vs those directly producing the outcome. This will allow the team to better understand dependencies and prioritize or align actions in a plan that lead to output. The supporting team must feed the actioning team. Often, the supporting area of expertise needs to work slightly ahead. In any given situation, there may be various layers of this sort of leap frogging that exist either internal or external to the team.

The supporting team and the actioning team should still work in parallel to ensure that collaboration is effective. In almost any case, there are at least some activities an actioning team can take prior to the supporting team closing key dependencies. Starting on some activities earlier will help the actioning team get out ahead of the problem. Disruptive leaders creatively figure out how to start on work as soon as possible so that they can set themselves up for success in the long run through incubation or hardening of existing outcomes.

Leaders shouldn't force teams to work or think too far ahead. Outcomes should be well defined. Actions that a team is going to take in the plan should be prioritized within a short working cycle. Short iterations or cycles of work allow the team to finish activities and adapt before starting on new action items.

Individuals on the team should commit to the action required to finish the cycle. They should also plan at least one or two cycles out. This forward planning should be done without a final commitment.

The lack of detailed obligation to future work establishes an expectation on and off the team that there are still some unknown factors. It also ensures that everyone involved is aware that known dependencies need to be considered. Short consistent work cycles and throttled commitments give the team room to navigate, understand the path forward, and still avoid the distraction of future work. This keeps team morale up and allows everyone to feel good that work is being completed in a measurable way. Focusing on the work in progress is especially helpful when impending activities or approach are somewhat unclear.

Teams often think about work items that might be further ahead in plan. Effective leaders capture these ideas as a living and breathing inventory of work to come. This is especially helpful when there are known activities that a team wants to capture early on as actions. The disruptive leader can then help facilitate a strategy and draw a line or correlation between the current working cycle and the longer-term outcome on the horizon. None the less, the team's commitment becomes exponentially important when action is decomposed into activities that can be achieved within the work cycle. At this point, the strategy and high-level framework that were once used to guide the team and decompose the plan now mean far less to the team working toward a committed iteration. The velocity by which the team is executing becomes the truth for what will be completed or achieved as an outcome.

Unrealistic goals and expectations can lead to a loss in momentum. Leaders who try to start work too quickly and without adequate resources will find themselves alone and defeated. In addition, teams that try to achieve an unrealistic velocity without careful consideration of what it will take to increase the tempo are also likely to fail.

Sometimes, teams, under pressure, will try to start too much work too early or too quickly. These teams pay for this mistake. This is a form of bad or unrealistic momentum. Even if the team is successful at starting quickly on too much work, their poorly planned initiative will lead to an unhealthy and unsustainable velocity. The disruptive leader knows that a team without the right resources and support is a team without a plan. This careless lack of discipline will leave the team crippled as individuals charge toward their goal unsupported or ill-equipped.

Teams that cut corners at the start of work are also more likely to lack integrity and discipline as they march forward toward an objective. Leaders will find that eventually a team under too much pressure to push through or solve a problem at any cost will simply try to cut more corners along the way.

Poor leaders will use phrases like "There is no excuse, get it done" and not carefully consider how that phrase may be translated or used to justify the means to an end. Worse yet, poor leaders, who themselves are under pressure, may not verify the team's actions or even purposely look the other way only to protect themselves from accountability.

Teams should never feel as if their leader has given them permission to "lie, cheat, and steal" from the start. Leaders themselves can't allow the team to justify bad behavior or not do the right thing in the name of getting the job done. Those who start work with a false sense of momentum are far more likely to engage in or continue with unethical activities as they move forward. They are also more likely to be aimless and ungrounded by a common objective. Pressure to perform at any cost is also much more likely to be interpreted and executed with individual behaviors that work against the collective interests of the team.

Instead, the disruptive leader moves forward carefully and helps the team commit only to work that is realistic. These individuals inspire the team to do the right thing and make incremental improvements along the way. The disruptive leader knows that it's important for the team to start work quickly, but, to do so carefully while fixated on the right goals and objective.

At a decisive moment or when faced with certain unknowns, a team may choose to add additional resources or even to focus all or most of its capacity on a single problem. When this is done, it has a much higher success rate when done as a group, and it must only be a focus of the team for a short period of time. Otherwise, the team risks spinning wildly out of control as it loses focus on the end goal to try and overcome an impossibility in the short term. This is also how a team can lose momentum and velocity all together as they waste valuable resources on a single blocker or problem for too long.

In some cases, the team may not even see the answer or an alternative if they focus too long on the same problem. Experts and specialists can lose sight of the bigger picture because they fail to objectively see how a situation is different from what they are expecting. This sort of failure is also common when a leader convinces the team to attack the same problem, in the same situation, with the same resources over and over. Failing repeatedly each time to achieve the objective, the team continues to hopelessly hit its head against the wall over and over hoping that sheer determination and willpower will help resolve the issue.

Leaders must help bring forward additional support, alter the plan, or even influence the situation if they want to see different results. The old saying is true, if you do the same thing over and over, expect to have the same results. Teams need to know that they have support available to them. Disruptive leaders work hard to ensure that the right partnerships are in place to help a team that is stuck or bogged down by issue.

Leaving a team working too far forward or stranded without the ability to get them additional support is yet another way that a leader can ensure failure. Teams should never feel desperate enough that they resort to determination and willpower as an answer to a problem except in the direst of circumstances. They should know their options and should feel free to exercise those options to solve a challenge or exploit an opportunity.

The minute a team begins to work toward a common goal, they need to be adaptive to the situation or environment. This flexibility is especially true when it comes to the individual tasks the team is completing along the way. If the team completes realistic goals and objectives early and often they are more likely to adapt and overcome challenges. Strategy and leadership can help pave the way by working out ahead of a team to keep them focused and unblocked. All too often, a poor leader or an inefficient team will try to work on activities that drag on with no end. In this scenario, completed activities can be plotted on a graph relatively flat over a duration before spiking abruptly at the end. This is a true tail sign that a team has failed to define their activity or objectives correctly. A team that can show consistent velocity by completing activities as it goes is a team that is sure to have the capacity to attack future goals as well. Teams that complete activity inconsistently end up with debt, discovery, and a barrage of unrealistic demands that lead to low morale and failure.

Leaders need to ensure that there is an appropriate balance of team members supporting vs team members actioning. Generally, a team that hasn't produced outcome is not a team that is really working. Leaders also need to validate that team members are working on the appropriate priorities. Each activity in the plan should have purpose. A team that works on too much planning, strategy, or the design without moving toward its final output is highly inefficient.

A leader must understand the team. Disruptive leaders know the roles, skills, or specialty of each team member. These leaders recognize responsibilities, potential, and limitations. Leaders must use each of these things, good or bad, as an advantage. Each team member has a super power and the disruptive leader knows how to find it and use it. They motivate individuals to take on activities that are the right fit for their skills or potential. Leaders must understand the individual's impact on the outcome if they are going to influence, coach, and advise.

This is also where partnership comes into play. Teams can't act alone. There are always going to be gaps in what they can think about, make, or do. Strong leaders understand this and work hard to develop external partnerships with other teams and individuals. A leader who has a good understanding of a team's capabilities before the work starts is one that will have no problem getting out ahead of the challenges the team may face. The disruptive leader keeps a strong network of partners and knows how to get support when the team needs it.

As a leader, we must do right by people. Sometimes that means giving up great resources to new opportunities or promotions that will benefit them. Over the years, I have helped many people on my teams move on to bigger and better things. I have always had far more satisfaction watching people soar as they go on to add more value in this world than they could of by doing what they were doing. To think that their accomplishments might have been, in part, influenced by a team they started on is an amazing feeling. This is also an important thing to consider whenever I look out across the team I might be leading in a given moment. Who will these folks become? How can I help them get there in this brief time we have together?

When someone moves on to bigger and better things, some might question their loyalty or mine for encouraging such behavior. The truth is that I have always believed it is far more likely people who move on to do great things will remain loyal to a team or a leader that stood by and supported them from the beginning. In fact, it has always been my experience, that these people simply add to the network of partners and alumni that can help a team influence on a much larger scale.

There is little reason to hold great people back in this world. In fact, it's downright counter-productive to keep people destined for greatness locked into something that isn't going to help them and help you. Often, these sorts of people on a team are already role models for others who want to add value as well.

High performers with loftier goals could be holding some people back who might otherwise step up and fill the role. When a strong resource leaves a team, they go on to be an important part of the team's network of outside alliances. They also continue to be a role model for others who might hope to someday achieve the same level of success. It is really a win all around for everyone. The team is given a benchmark and it can ride the wake of success left behind. In addition, the leader can strengthen the team's outside partnerships by supporting or encouraging the jump toward a new horizon for a high performing member of the team.

Leaders must work hard to make sure that team members with specific skills or abilities are given the right opportunities to be successful. Great leaders challenge the team, yet, they also put people in a role where they can succeed. Great leaders coach and advise team members and help them discover individual strengths, capabilities, and potential. These leaders also know how to use partners to help a team win when there is a gap. They look for opportunities to engage with partners and bring them in at the right moment. The disruptive leader aggressively influences the roles and responsibilities on the team. Their influence is an art that takes a great deal of practice. These leaders are great at making sure the right capability, resource, or partner is front and center at the right time to help super charge a team.

Even in a difficult and confusing situation where partnership seems impossible or restricted by a larger organization, leaders should still seek to take advantage of any possible opportunity they can, to get all the help the team needs. Great leaders aren't afraid to get help. Successful teams welcome and embrace all the help they can. Finding help takes courage and initiative. Disruptive leaders never wait for help or assume someone will provide it. They take initiative to get help and solve problems. They also inspire individuals on the team to do the same.

Ideal situations are rare. Risks and issues are hard to plan for. However, challenges should not stop a team or leader from taking initiative or starting to work on a plan. Partnerships can help a team jump start a plan, solve for a skills gap, or even reduce risk over the long term. Opportunities for partnership are everywhere.

Great leaders don't assume that they are fulfilling their roles and responsibilities by staying within a certain position among the pack. Instead, they help the team seek out opportunities to be more effective and decisive.

Internal partnerships within an organization or even within a single team where resources are cross-trained and more deeply collaborating are obvious things to exploit. However, even when these partnerships fall within the sphere of influence a leader has, they are still very difficult to coordinate.

When a team is well equipped with the right resources and an adequate timeline to work on activities, it may be easy to complete goals and objectives at a high velocity. On the other hand, all too often, teams "fail together" if there is a struggle to partner across roles or disciplines. In these situations, a leader can use all the help they can get to drive a team toward more effective collaboration.

A team that struggles to partner internally often sees lower quality output and a much lower velocity than a team adept at collaboration. Sometimes this means that individuals are in the wrong roles or that certain capabilities on the team are not being leveraged appropriately. This may create friction and miss-trust on the team. Leaders must work closely together to align output across various roles or responsibilities. This alignment requires strong communication, intellectual support, and a strong diplomatic defense of rules or standards. Without the right expectation or alliance in place on the team between each craft or discipline that is represented, the team will likely step on each other's toes.

To gain alignment, groups within teams may need to form and appoint trusted leads to help matrix roles and responsibilities diplomatically across an organization. Successful teams appoint liaisons to help facilitate communication, thought leadership, or enforcement of standards.

The disruptive leader uses the liaison to shield themselves from having to face, think about, or deal with outside rules that might distract or weigh down the team. Great leaders recognize and rely on liaisons to help facilitate collaboration on the team with external forces that require certain behaviors. The liaison serves as a point person for each group within or outside of the team.

Each partnership should have a single point of contact that functions as a liaison between leaders, the team, and the partnership. Leaders who lean on liaisons in a partnership are far more successful at gaining trust within the team. The liaison can help make sure that communication is working, they can help keep the initial stages of a plan on schedule, and they can influence strategy or planning along the way by thinking out ahead of individual team members focused on more tactical activities. More importantly, a liaison can help track down and coordinate support for the team at critical times.

Liaisons are leaders themselves who can help identify issues with dependency and timing on a team. Liaisons, as a disruptive leader on the team, take the initiative to help ensure that internal and external team members are unblocked. They themselves can coach specialized resources through issues and coordinate or identify dependencies that are not being met. They also help to enforce rules, norms, and standards on the team by pointing out when team members from an internal or external partnership are not being used effectively.

When a team begins to work on a plan, the situation can become confusing and stressful. There are a lot of things that individuals and leaders must pay attention to. Liaison's provide real time interaction as an advisor. The liaison can help translate or improve information and communication exchanged between various roles. This role also helps to facilitate moments when there is a handoff of responsibilities between partners and a team.

The disruptive leader ensures that liaisons are effective and successful. These leaders build trust by facilitating a transparent working relationship with the liaison. They also stress open and real-time dialog around intended output and key dependencies.

Simply put, liaisons should have a clear view of scope, timing, and budget constraints influencing the team. Without this information, the liaison cannot respond effectively to requests from leaders or other team members. It is important for leaders to remember that liaisons seldom have all the above information unless it has been given to them. Even when they do have information, they don't have all the answers. Meaning, there will be things a liaison can see, advise, and help influence, but, they can't control the outcome entirely or see every potential issue.

Teams need to be aware of resource constraints. Leaders need to help facilitate a culture which recognizes that support from a liaison or craft is not unlimited. It should be prioritized to target big problems. Teams should have just enough cross-functionality that individual members can solve small problems end to end themselves. The disruptive leader recognizes that too much interdependence is not a good way of organizing, leading, or working.

Leaders and team members who rely on a support partnership should work closely with the liaison to standardize communication and requests. Repeatable activities should be easy to ask for, simple, and clear. In fact, for smaller less complex efforts the duration, scope, and type of request should be well known and repeatable. This is not the easiest thing for any organization to accomplish. It's very easy, when defining repeatable process, to become complacent or miss-placed in terms of how a request is used. This is where leaders should rely on and trust the liaison who can help navigate or adjust a request when it is not adequate for a given situation.

All of this means that liaisons are often generalists as much as they are strategists. They maintain a mutual familiarity of each craft on the team to ensure that requests are not impossible, unnecessary, or unsuitable. Liaisons also appreciate the problems that each team member or its leadership faces as well. They are the tried and true advisor for their own discipline. In the end, the liaison is another disruptive leader on the team whose partnership is critical for any team's success.

Leaders should ensure that each individual team member can complete end to end task with limited to no support. On the other hand, when limited support is available, leaders can apply it to larger problems as a means of collaboration and partnership. Liaisons should be a part of the team with a completely transparent view of the strategy, plan, and work. Planning and requirements should be pre-defined to guide a partner and keep them focused. To be effective, partnerships must be moral, reciprocal, confident, and friendly.

Measure Results

Teams that are always measuring typically learn and adapt much easier than those who don't. The highly successful team consistently measures progress against objectives. They also assess the resources necessary to work toward a common goal. Leaders of a disruptive team capture feedback continuously from those around them. They keep a close eye on insights gathered from the team's environment to help make effective decisions or to understand necessary changes.

Teams also measure their own consistency to improve efficiency and create the right culture for individuals to operate effectively. Leaders utilize the lessons learned from working together to evolve expectations. They also influence and inspire team members. The disruptive leader believes in a predictable culture built on common values, beliefs, and emotions.

Successful teams also tend to use a variety of sensing techniques or available technologies to monitor their environment. Even when something they see isn't obvious or clear, these teams then have multiple sources of data at their disposal for analogical reasoning or assumption building.

Leaders listen and process the information that they gather. They understand that the data they are gathering from experiences and the environment around them is helping to make more effective decisions. Leaders also measure to help establish a direction for the team. They use the information gathered to help validate theories and prioritize efforts more impactfully.

Testing is not only a tool that helps a team improve quality, it is also a way of measuring. For example, a team can test the impact of their work and, in turn, learn just enough to make critical decisions before moving forward. Concepting is one form of this testing that can help a team validate a hypothesis to make the right measured decision.

It goes without saying that many of my clients in the insurance and financial sectors tend to get this sort of an approach more than anyone. They don't often face disruption in the same way that some companies do because quite honestly many of them feel that they are too big to fail. Yet, they are always testing and learning. Their financial acumen means that they like to go by the numbers before deciding on anything. This can be bad as it does often slow them down or hold them back, but, they are much better at using a scientific method to test the waters.

I have spent a great deal of time helping them build better decisioning engines and marketing platforms capable of incredible feats of automation or cognitive reasoning, but, I am always impressed by the fact that even small changes can have a profound impact when executed at scale.

The challenge with most financial institutions is that they have many cooks in the kitchen on any one project. Security and protecting personal data are critical, performance of systems is non-negotiable, and business outcomes must be well aligned across the organization. Even when a team can prove the value of something and quantify it, they may not always get all the stars aligned to approve the go ahead. Many financial institutions or insurance providers struggle with the fact that they have so much data and so many systems working at scale. It's hard to rally multiple internal or even external teams to get the job done.

I have always had a lot of success creating integrated working teams that bring stakeholders together on a regular basis to discuss strategy and plans before they are submitted or approved. Even when there is wide spread disagreement or dissention, these teams bring attention to certain topics and make approval or momentum easier to achieve downstream. Keeping conversations out of the weeds is a key tactic. People are far less likely to stop listening or argue and it's easier to pivot when something becomes non-negotiable.

Many of the same rules that might apply to a team working toward an outcome or specific project would apply to a working committee operating at a much higher level. They may never produce the outcome, but, they could create artifacts that influence whether a team or resources are approved to work on something that is important to a leader or group.

That said, the working team can slow down progress if expectations are not appropriately managed. Sometimes, they can demand too much measurement or testing before agreeing on or aligning to a strategy. When this happens, I have always had far more success when I have pushed to have something tangible completed that gives them reason or motivation to approve additional efforts. A proof of concept or even a small proof of success in a production environment can go a long way toward helping senior leaders understand that they are missing out on a potential outcome.

Disruptive leaders can't let measurement and testing hold them back from moving forward. In other words, disruptive leaders don't wait. They don't wait for direction, for permission, for anything. They take the initiative. They get there first. At the onset of any work cycle, it is critical that a team kicks off with as high a velocity as it can. The first to the table with a reasonable plan often wins. Teams that can use their initial velocity to create something that helps prove or validate the plan often are the first to secure freedom of action in their environments. Leaders who work toward an initial concept quickly and efficiently create confidence and trust. Front loaded momentum can propel a team toward success. It could even help the larger organization or supporting teams move in a more focused direction with confidence. Concepts can validate a high risk and high value element of the plan or a hypothesis that makes the team more comfortable with timing going forward.

Leaders don't wait to start work and they don't wait to start partnering or collaborating either. Liaisons and supporting roles on the team should be involved in the work from day one. Whether leaders are working toward an understanding of the problem or they are still defining the strategy, it is never too early to involve partners. Partnerships across various disciplines from the start create stability on the team.

Disruptive leaders don't wait until there is an immediate need or issue to act. When the process in an organization indicates that a need is probable, liaisons and leaders should be gathered to discuss. When an understanding is reached, teams should be prepared and dispatched to ensure momentum.

Leaders don't need to wait because they already have direction in mind from the moment a team forms. In fact, teams that spend time conceptualizing their goal, early on, are more likely to be successful at building momentum in the right direction. Even if more specific activity or definition has hardly started, it is important for the team to have some proven or hypothetical working model of what they are about to do.

Disruptive leaders will start with a concept to help the team lift the fog of a situation. These leaders will typically focus the team's effort on an assumption or hypothesis. The team should look for a question that they can validate or prove. Leaders may also choose to visualize or demonstrate the larger plan in one form or another so that the team can step through it.

Disruptive leaders understand that a conceptual view of a plan or its end state will help to shape a clearer understanding of the outcome. A concept could include a demonstration of the plan in a mock environment, an outline, a proof, a model, or something else altogether. No matter what method or approach the team takes as it creates a concept, their goal should be to establish a base of knowledge. This will help the team understand next steps and navigate a challenging situation or environment more clearly.

Teams that work on or take part in an initial concept may be a bit smaller or leaner than the final team that begins execution, however, these teams can still help to establish momentum across all roles that may ramp up on the team downstream. As the concept is finalized and demonstrated, the scope takes shape. The team then grows in organization to resemble what it will look like as work continues. The closer a team gets to kicking off, the more real the team should start to look. This means that by the time work starts, it can start with great speed and velocity.

As the team works toward completing objectives, they will reduce the risk or impact of unknown factors in the plan. With each demo or demonstration of work in progress, the team will get closer to a sustainable outcome. The disruptive leader recognizes that iteration and continuous validation of the team's goals allows for momentum to build around the outcome as well. Internal and external teams are more likely to believe in, embrace, and adopt the output of the team if they have had access to versions or variations of it along the way. This is especially true if external teams or influences can provide feedback.

Teams that stick too closely to a defined approach for staffing, defining, planning, and executing are punished by the unknown. Risks, issues, blockers, and change are inevitable. Disruptive leaders don't let their own ego stand in the way when they kick off work with a team. They know that rigid checklists that don't consider the situation will cause a team to lose momentum and likely sacrifice quality over the long run. A challenging start for a team is often the spider that made the web. In the end, unrelated issues a team faces months or years down the road can often be traced back to a rocky start.

The leader earns trust internally and externally during the early stages of work. The disruptive leader knows that a concept or an early demonstration of progress will create believers on and off the team. The idea of starting, when work is likely, yet not approved is bold. Initiating something without permission or approval can be risky. Great leaders take chances like this because they know that the payoff is worth it. At the same time, leaders are still accountable and must remain so when they ask or facilitate such risk. If a leader is wrong, then they need to own it. Poor leaders who take risks like this will blame their teams or liaisons for the chance they took. Accepting accountability for how work starts and not just how it ends isn't easy, but it must be measured and culturally embedded in every organization.

It is worth noting that starting early can make it harder for a team to change direction. Teams can get overly focused on an assumption and miss the bigger picture when they conceptualize the plan before execution. Momentum is a two-way street. Once a concept sets the team in motion toward an objective, a leader will have a harder time navigating risks, issues, and changes. The more velocity a team has toward a tactical plan, the harder it can be to steer it in a new direction.

None the less, great teams are not just measured by the quality of their results, the efficiency of execution, but, by the tenacity at which they start and the innovation that they spark early in the lifecycle of work.

Leaders must ensure that their teams are organized in a flexible structure. Team organization should effectively allow for scale, collaboration, and partnership. Teams must work toward an outcome or a common goal. Leaders must ensure that the team understands the intent of its outcome and the strategy by which the plan is based.

Disruptive leaders remove blockers for the team that prevent them from understanding or pushing forward. These leaders make sure that the team has the right resources in place, needs are taken care of, and there is a plan in place to keep them well fed with new work as they progress. Lastly, but perhaps most important, disruptive leaders maintain high morale.

Pageantry can help to ensure that the team understands expectations. A team with an exciting and predictable culture will likely maintain high morale and attract better partners. Leaders know how to tap into the positive emotions of a team to establish the right amount of pomp and circumstance around a team's ceremonies so that they are widely adopted. Pageantry leads to culture and a legacy that a team can use to inspire and motivate its future generations. Again though, the disruptive leader is empathetic and doesn't use pageantry to manipulate the team. Instead, these leaders see it as a silent partner helping to create a sense of community around a common interest that a team shares. Pageantry will take shape over time. As the team unites toward a common goal, their ceremony will evolve and stabilize to a point where they share more than just common values, beliefs, or interests.

Because the disruptive leader is empathetic, they are also merciful. These leaders make it easier for new team members or outsiders to assimilate with the team, but, they are not overly oppressive. They recognize or appreciate individual differences and respect them. These leaders know that there is more than one way to solve a problem or perceive a situation and that helps them appreciate others who may have an opposing view or a different style of work.

The disruptive leader understands the power of telling a good story. They will humanize the culture and weave predictable events or expectations into consistent ceremonies on the team. These leaders use stories about work past, present, and future to bolster a belief in the team and its plan.

The team should meet consistently and with purpose. Values, beliefs, and norms will become widely adopted on a team over time. Disruptive leaders recognize that groups within teams will form for short periods of time to complete a small number of tasks or spark change. These small groups will likely not adopt their own pageantry or culture unless they scale and stick around. The intelligent leader will make it easier for smaller teams to lean on or use a larger set of values, beliefs, and norms as a guide. Ceremonial procedures stay out of the weeds. They are grand gestures that help keep a team unified. The team will handle the details and form habits from a ritualized cadence that keeps them on task even when the details of the plan are undocumented.

Ceremonies are mutually agreed upon by a team. They establish a pattern for working that can help to keep team members unblocked and ahead of risk. When team members understand expectations, they can predict next steps and put more focus into solving problems that deviate from the norm. This makes it easier to change the plan or handle issues when they come up. When ceremonies are working, everyone knows what to do if there is a change or an issue. They know how to plug in, fill the role they are assigned, and they generally agree with or support the process by which these things are handled.

No matter what, effective ceremonies are flexible and adaptable to the environment or situation in which a team is working. Rigid process may help to establish rigor for a team, but it can also stifle a team's ability to handle change or adapt to the unknown. What was acceptable in one environment may eventually go out of style or not make sense when conditions change. Teams must adapt and tweak their ceremonies to stay relevant without losing a sense of culture or identity.

It goes without saying that leaders and teams must communicate and collaborate to be effective. Social contracts within a team that define common values or that create standards lay the foundation for effective communication. Teams will harness standards to more efficiently communicate when a challenging situation takes shape.

The implicit and explicit rules by which the team will work together should be clear and well understood. This understanding starts with spending time together. Time spent together on and off the team can help break down barriers and build trust within the ceremony of the team. Teams need to meet more often, and leaders need to engage with teams frequently. Disruptive leaders recognize the need to be present and available for the team whenever possible.

Leaders must enforce ceremonies and make sure that they are continuous. Pageantry is not just something that happens at the beginning or end of a cycle. Planning and adaptation, for example, are continuous activities that a team makes time for.

Planning is done within the construct of a working cycle which is defined based on calendar or time increments. A predefined and standardized work cycle will limit how many activities are defined at any one time. This method ensures that the team is not overloaded with actions they are expected to commit to or work at any given moment. Leaders must be great score keepers. Disruptive leaders have an almost clairvoyant ability to understand and perceive time, its limitations, and its opportunities. This ability helps them coach teams through planning and commitment to action.

Because small teams can only work on just a few actions ahead at any one point in time, it is important to limit the agenda of a planning ceremony so that the team only focuses on current or near-term activities. In fact, the planning ceremony should mainly be used to plan one or two work cycles ahead. However, other ceremonies may exist to create larger strategies and longer-term plans that look much further out with an understanding that they may change. Leaders should use a strategy to guide longer term planning.

It is ok to capture future work when it is identified. High-level actions can be prioritized way out ahead of where the team is currently working. Regular prioritization is one of the foundational things a team does together to stay focused. As a ceremony, prioritization allows a team to meet often and review potential future work.

Defined actions and priorities may fluctuate. The targeted fidelity of a goal or objective may also change. Leaders enforce collaboration on the team and use defined ceremonies to manage this change. Every member of a team should understand what the process is to review and adjust activities over time.

Change, of course, is not the only factor impacting actions. Dependency is also an important element that a leader must consider. Special care should be given to create ceremonies for the team that focus on ensuring dependency is well aligned. Disruptive leaders recognize that dependencies need to be monitored and communicated so that the team can adjust its plan appropriately.

Leaders also make sure that their teams are always learning. They establish a cadence of regular touchpoints for the team to share what they have learned. Whenever a plan has cycled through execution or the team has completed an objective, there should be retrospective around what went well, what didn't, and what could be improved in future iterations. This sort of ceremony is critical for a team to grow and learn from success or failure.

Continuous review and control of quality is a critical ceremony as well. Teams use reviews of the work and subsequent discussions to hold each other accountable. They also validate that there are clear acceptance criteria for defined actions. The disruptive leader continuously enforces ceremonies that allow the team to meet, discuss, and validate quality.

Leaders help the team establish a consistent cadence for each ceremony. This tempo sets the pace for collaboration, communication, and work. The capacity of the team and the rate under which the team can or should execute action are both considerations for what the standardized cadence should be. Tempo establishes a rhythm under which leaders can understand and even predict the rate at which a plan will be executed, and an outcome achieved.

Even though the team is executing effectively and efficiently using a defined ceremony, leaders must take care to ensure that the team does not become complacent. Success can create a false sense of security for a team. Leaders must continue to look out ahead and ensure that work is being validated along the way. The disruptive leader ensures that the team is continuing to learn new skills, and that individuals are advancing their craft. Teams also need to continue to take the time to consider alternative options, measure their success, and avoid reaching an outcome before their work products are ready.

Disruptive leaders need to make sure that every approach the team takes is elastic and well suited for change. Leaders can utilize a repeatable framework of defined ceremonies to help ensure that a team is less vulnerable to risk or issues as they work. The situation and the working environment dictate strategy, approach, and plan. However, the ceremonies a team uses make sure that the resulting work efforts are well defined, in a timely manner, to effectively manage the obscurity of a situation.

Great leaders understand the need for ceremony and they also work hard to make sure that each team member is working with the right resources, knowledge of the plan, and in good spirit or high morale. There is no single organization, solution, or plan that can accomplish this by itself. No defined methodology or rigorous process can solve for all the ceremonial needs a team might have. Strong leaders are not fundamentalists who are married to a specific ideology. They instead know how to let the situation evolve the social contract of the team and its working ceremony without sacrificing quality. The ability to see out ahead of the work in progress is a skill that will help a good leader understand the value of this concept.

A strong leader understands the need for feedback. Feedback is something that a great leader is always measuring and monitoring. Feedback doesn't have to be negative. Disruptive leaders know how to embrace positive feedback and use contingency to exploit a success rather than to redeem a failure. Furthermore, even when contingency is used to fix a situation, more resources do not always solve the problem. In fact, more resources will likely make the problem worse or produce far less outcome. This may sound counter-intuitive, but this knowledge is one of the things that really separates a good leader from a bad one. Disruptive leaders will use feedback and contingency as tools to help their existing team build more momentum at a critical moment in the plan.

In this way, feedback can help to identify not just a risk or an issue but also an opportunity. Most importantly, feedback can help a team find the low hanging fruit. This includes the things that they can easily influence without a lot of effort. This is where leaders can take advantage of their reserves to exploit feedback they are measuring.

Rather than using contingency to solve a problem or a failure, good leaders look for weakness and exploit it. To the disruptive leader, failure and weakness are two very different things. Weakness is redeemable with enhancement or hardening. An example might be, if a plan is behind and failing to achieve its outcome, the team might decide to harden what it already has and release this as a potential solution rather than apply more resources to try and catch up to plan or extend the timeline altogether.

Teams that understand how to exploit weakness will ignore the strong parts of their work temporarily to rapidly address the weak ones. This allows a team to take advantage of what they already have without needing more, additional, or new output.

Teams can then wait to deal with work that hasn't completed yet. The more challenging needs or items that are behind plan are then gradually reduced. They are less important because weaker capabilities have been enhanced to solve the problem.

Sometimes the team itself doesn't have to address weakness. An example of an exception would be borrowed time and resources that belong to a partner or external team. In some cases, other teams can invest, for their own mutual benefit, at no cost to the existing team. However, when this isn't possible, Feedback and contingency can be used hand in hand to exploit weakness.

Using feedback as a tool for exploiting opportunity is not easy. Priority can be confusing for a leader or a team. Outside pressure to meet a deadline or a misunderstanding of the end state can add to the chaos. Outsiders within the organization or external to it will rarely know exactly what opportunities can be exploited, how feedback should be used, or even what work exists that can be hardened and enhanced based on the feedback.

Disruptive leaders do not rely on liaisons, outside support, or outside organizations to make final decisions about what opportunities to exploit related to feedback. The team needs to be accountable or responsible for doing the right thing with the feedback it has or opportunities that are identified. Outsiders will have an impossible time understanding the full picture of what a team is facing, and their decision will be largely ineffective. Disruptive leaders are steadfast in their resolve and remain unaffected by the negative pressure they receive from the outside.

Transparency can go a long way toward ensuring that advisors or partners have the information they need to help leaders take advantage of feedback. Advisors can serve as trainers or navigators on a team when they fully understand the situation and environment a team is facing. These partners can help the team mature existing capabilities before moving too far forward in executing an overall strategy.

Achieving maturity in this way is often risky. A partner can't always bail a team out of a tough situation by helping to train resources. There may be far more than a skills gap holding back the team from resolving issues it knows or understands exist. Chances are, there are many reasons why a team hasn't matured to take on certain tasks. For example, the team could be blocked by various dependencies or they might be jumping from issue to issue putting out fires which are contributing to slowing them down.

Sometimes, poor leaders might miss-interpret the reason why their team is held back and unable to overcome certain challenges identified as feedback. The path forward or changes required to remediate feedback could even seem obvious. Miss-guided leaders might dedicate reserves to a partner hoping to close a skills gap only to run into some of the same problems again. Contingency given to or used by an advisor or partner can't be expected to solve a bottleneck like this. In fact, a bottleneck is exactly the sort of issue that will be made worse by a leader who tries to throw more resources from the outside at a problem to solve it.

Feedback isn't always a good thing. It can stall a team's progress, so, leaders must make sure that it is appropriately prioritized. Too much time should never be lost enhancing or hardening existing capabilities. Exploiting an opportunity and using contingency to address a weakness requires a delicate balance of "just enough" for "just the right amount of time" to achieve an outcome "just in time". Otherwise, success in using feedback will be limited.

As a rule of thumb, leaders must facilitate a compromise between lateral and forward exploitation of an opportunity. In other words, a balance must exist between the enhancement of an existing capability before exploiting the benefits of a new one. Disruptive leaders understand when a team should push forward, and they help advise or coach resources to use what they have or seek new opportunity.

The speed at which an output is reached or the general velocity of work completed are usually the two most critical things that an individual team member can help to influence. These are also the two things that are most useful to everyone else in the organization or team. When individuals themselves are motivated correctly to focus on these two elements, the team strengthens weakness which in turn makes it easier to exploit more difficult challenges.

When one team member moves slower than another or one team slower than another team, leaders must facilitate the movement of individuals away from what they had planned to do. Instead, they should be guided toward the hardening and enhancement of what is already completed. This can also help to give the team time to solve a blocking issue or dependency that may have prevented other team members from advancing.

On the other hand, additional support from new resources or existing team members should not be applied to work in progress to help increase the velocity. It should harden and enhance what exists not try to speed up the effort of what doesn't. Boundaries between roles, responsibilities, and commitment exist to prevent the team from stepping on the toes of others. Leaders must make sure that these lines are not crossed.

The framework by which the work or roles are defined exists to make executing the work more convenient. When team members are assigned the same task, the boundary is a hindrance. Wrongly guided cross-functional pairs on a team can take quite a toll on morale. It can also impact the team's ability to collaborate effectively.

When a team member or a team is ahead in plan, they should continue forward so long as other teams or team members are there to back them up. Feedback is an effective tool to exploit work completed through enhancement or hardening while a team waits to advance. When enough momentum is achieved, the team can then continue forward and complete additional work. Every effort should be made then to use any available time to unblock team members or teams who may have some dependency preventing them from keeping up.

Leaders never stop learning. They are great listeners because of this. Disruptive leaders listen not just to their own teams, but they pay attention to what is going on around them on other teams as well. They constantly tweak their point of view and re-align their approach. Disruptive leaders pick up new skills, learn from those around them, and look out into the future to understand what they should be thinking about next.

Leaders who listen, understand that it is important to look at what competitors are doing, how technology is changing, or even understanding how operational models are evolving. They should ask the same of their teams. These leaders make sure that each individual team member makes time for not just learning but listening. It's one thing to pick up new skills here and there or practice a craft to improve on it but it's another thing altogether to listen. Listening helps a team focus or re-orient itself if off track. Listening puts bias aside for a moment and replaces it with empathy and mercy.

Leaders who have empathy tend to make great listeners. They are better at putting aside their own view to try and understand a situation. Leaders like this are usually not fundamentalists either. They don't walk around worried too much about the plan or a process that isn't quite as expected. This makes them more likely to be successful.

In general, leaders always seek information. They want to answer questions like: "Are there any risks or dependencies that we haven't thought about? Are my assumptions valid? What are other teams doing? It looks like my own team didn't finish a task yet, what does that really mean?" Answers to questions like these come from listening. Whether that is physically listening to what a team member, customer, or stakeholder is saying, or it is monitoring and tracking what is being reported both explicitly and implicitly.

Disruptive leaders harness analytics to process a situation and actuate a response. Analytics capture the context of each event. At-scale, this data helps leaders understand actions, behaviors, intent, and trend lines. Reports aggregate this information into a story to help leaders understand not just the status of a plan or movement toward an objective, but, the situation that a team is facing. Measured analytics can be used to predict future behavior, trends, or change. It can also identify morale issues, risks, or other unhealthy elements plaguing a team at work.

Testing is the one tool that every leader has at their disposal to listen. Disruptive leaders monitor various quality metrics to check and validate the world around them. They are always testing their environment or the situation to understand more about it. Often, these leaders will start with a question about what is acceptable or assumed. The test data can then inform how far off from a baseline or expected trend the team or its output really are.

Teams navigating the unknown should follow the same steps any good analyst or scientist would take to answer a question. They should research things first, establish a hypothesis, conduct a test or experiment to validate that hypothesis, look at the data, adjust their theory and communicate the results.

Testing to validate a hypothesis gives the team confidence and allows them to determine a course of action. Working is a form of testing. By just starting on something a team can make the decision to test an approach. Successful teams understand that each person on a team is a tester and that everyone, together, is constantly learning by testing the world around them.

The disruptive leader is an enabler who can advise a team to operationalize the results of testing. It's one thing to work toward validating something but it's another thing all together to act on what was learned from a test. It can be difficult to know what to do with that information. The entire team must work together within the defined process to continuously adapt appropriately to what any one person may have learned.

Leaders help the team execute activities to optimize, change, or maintain a situation. This sort of thing happens in near real time every day on a team in various ways. Leaders must check the work, talk to customers or stakeholders, and communicate what they know or learn back to the broader team.

Sometimes a team can operate successfully despite other problems just because they are actively listening to what is going on around them. Even in the face of obscurity, difficult work, and an unfavorable situation, a team that is actively listening or seeking out feedback in one way or another, early and often, is a team that likely will evolve and adapt to meet or exceed expectations.

It goes without saying that listening is an activity that requires serious virtue. Leaders who rely on individual team members to test and validate an outcome, oversee work in progress, and have the end user or customer's best interest in mind must ensure that they have good people in place to execute any sort of monitoring like this. Integrity, desire to do the right thing, and an ability to push back or navigate competing interests are all important characteristics for those leaders who are tasked with listening.

Leaders themselves should never just rely on the team to test, monitor, or collect and solicit feedback. They too must know the end user or customer. They themselves must measure results visibly and validate progress. This allows the team to correct errors from the past, prepare for prompt or effective change, and anticipate the future.

A situation can change quickly and without warning. This sort of rapid change requires fast thinking and decision making. Leaders must be prepared and willing to accept change as a normal way of working. Teams who fail to adapt and leaders who try to stick to closely to a plan are doomed to fail.

That said, commitments made by a team or decisions facilitated by a leader should not change on a whim. The reason for change should be heavily weighted on the need to adapt to an evolving situation. None the less, every team faces the need to adapt their plan or consider a new approach toward the work before they can move forward. Sometimes that means shifting direction before work has even started.

When change happens, leaders must coach their teams beyond irritation and a rather instinctive tendency to question or critique the shift in plan. This sort of criticism can have a huge impact on the morale of the team. Leaders who use language that makes it easier for the team to adapt in any situation are more likely to help influence the level of irritation a team feels when things change. The same is true for process and workflow on the team. When change is an agreed upon and accepted thing and there is a set method for reacting to and handling it then the team is less likely to question or criticize. One-way leaders can facilitate change is to establish reviews of the plan where the team constantly meets to discuss activities, quality, commitments, feedback, and dependency risks. When any one of those topics is reviewed, change is certain to be discussed.

The intake or definition of new work serves as the eyes and ears of a small team. Methods to add, ideate, or re-imagine work activities keep the team marching toward a common goal. Reviewing and cleansing the existing plan keeps the work relevant. Teams measure their success by understanding first what work needs to be done. Acceptance of that work can be defined by facilitating meetings to review the work in the context of the most current situation that the team is facing.

Sometimes the act of reviewing future efforts in the context of activities that are in progress, feedback received, or even past lessons learned could uncover an opportunity for the team. More often though, a team that constantly meets to discuss the current situation and the plan only turn up negative information. Discussion around trends, risks, issues, blockers, or discovery can often feel very negative to a team and its leadership. A disruptive leader knows all too well that a team should never allow itself to become discouraged from reporting or discussing information that might feel negative.

In fact, leaders should never fear bad news or avoid it. Its best to take bad news head on quickly and transparently. Often, the negative comes with a silver lining or an opportunity that can be exploited. A loss becomes a win, or a failure turns out to be a success when looked at more objectively. Unlike a fine wine, bad news rarely gets better with age.

The intelligent leader finds bad news to be of the utmost importance. Leaders who embrace this idea and stress upon their teams the need to report early and often find more success than those who try to hide information. Disruptive leaders encourage dialog around bad news even when it feels negative.

Meeting to cleanse or adjust the plan is an active method of listening. Leaders should never lose sight of the value that continuous discovery has for a team as they execute. Listening and learning can come from research, analysis, or discussion around the work that the team is performing or the work they could perform in the future.

That said, a leader must never allow listening activities to degenerate into a routine, careless, you-do-it sort of activity. Disruptive leaders should be hands on when it comes to continuous discovery and adjustment of a plan. The amount of research, analysis, or review is highly dependent on the situation. It is also possible to over indulge in discovery activities or the act of cleansing potential work activities.

Too much assessment or discussion can stall a team. Too many meetings can over load or distract from the task at hand. Leaders who take up too much valuable time can feel controlling. The art of coaching a team toward a solution is then lost. This doesn't mean though that adjustment to plan and discovery are not critical for success. In fact, even if there is no apparent reason to do it at all, do it anyway. Like so many of these things, the "just enough" rule of thumb is always a good measure for any leader to follow.

Discovery and adjustment of the plan will by its very nature cause or even enable change. It is an error for any leader to assume that change on its own indicates a lack of resolution to a problem or goal. Leaders must navigate this very carefully. They must ensure that the team feels like it is making solid progress against goals that are accomplishable. At the same time, leaders must also foster a working environment that embraces discovery and adaptation. Change should be regarded as normal, happily accepted, and communicated with an air of confidence.

Inspire Courage

Leaders are bold, but they also inspire courage as well. The greatest leaders do this by example. These individuals know how to turn pageantry into a long-standing culture. They leave a legacy for others to follow. Over time, their teams adopt various practices in their absence or long after they are gone.

Teams that put time and energy into things that are repeatable or things that can accelerate their progress are more successful in the long run. Re-usability gives teams an edge that helps to make them more focused and energized. Disruptive leaders put more value on the things that make a situation different and less on what makes it the same.

Years ago, while working with a consumer product and manufacturing company, I was tasked with picking up the pieces after a large scale roll out of a new storefront was delayed. One of the first things I discovered was the fact that the marketing and business team were unprepared for the pending release. In part, their lack of acceptance and understanding of the technology was delaying change during an organizational transformation. Prior to my arrival, leaders within the organization had hoped that new and exciting technology capabilities would spark or inspire change. Instead, the transformation was met with a disappointing resistance from various business users.

My work began with an understanding of the situation and it then continued with coaching and training around various tools or process that needed to be adopted or planned for. Each marketer on the team needed to re-imagine their role in the context of both the technology capabilities and the broader campaign we would launch after the release.

There were several existing templates that I already had from previous experiences that I could apply to the situation, but, each one needed to be tweaked so that the team would understand them. From a maturity standpoint, it was critical to establish a mode of crawl, walk, and run. Rather than forcing the team to run right out of the gate, I needed to adjust behaviors slowly. They needed to feel as if change was possible. Each marketer and merchant on the team also had to accept that everything in their current world was doable even if that meant that it was executed in a new way. The team needed to lift and shift their work on existing platforms to the new ones and they needed to be prepared to take advantage of new capabilities that were rolling out.

It was a lot for each team member to take in. To them, it felt like so much change at one time. I simplified a core set of things that they could learn from and adapt to over time. New process, templates, or general ways of working were tested and adapted. We met regularly to discuss the changes and we adjusted some things so that everyone felt comfortable.

After a short while, I no longer needed to help the team. A few leaders found the courage to help others adjust. Once they got the hang of things and began to use the simplified and repeatable tools I had created to accelerate their learning curve, they began to adapt on their own. This meant that I really didn't need to show them every detail or train on every aspect of the new system. I had to inspire them to want to change and I had to give them just enough to get started. Once they had enough of an edge, the team propelled itself way beyond anywhere I could have taken it on my own.

An edge is leverage, but, the intelligent leader also recognizes it as a tool that lets a team stand out or stand on its own. In this way, teams themselves begin to own their own destiny. Leaders who inspire fearlessness also enable miracles. These miracles are moments where a few highly motivated individuals can overcome great odds to get something done. Moments like this only further fuel the culture of the team. Leaders take advantage of behaviors and emotions. They also use boundaries and the momentum of work to their advantage. Disruptive leaders inspire tenaciousness and optimism to motivate each individual team member.

As a team works together, it will develop a sense of culture. Leaders who coach their teams toward predictable, transparent, and accepted norms can help to establish a social contract among members of the team. This contract will serve to govern behavior through common values and ideas that the collective team shares. In its simplest form, a culture will grow as a team works toward a common goal and collaborates day after day. There is inherently commonality in sharing the trials and tribulations of working together. The consistent tempo and ritual of a team's ceremonies will set the standard for individuals to find common ground.

At the same time, culture can dull or erode over time as new ideas or changing situation segments the team into different camps. Disruptive leaders know how to use this as an opportunity to unite the organization. Division and competition can be as much a tool for uniting a team in the long run as it can be a way of boosting morale among segments of the group individually.

Morale is an important factor in sustaining cultural values and beliefs. The lower the morale, the more likely it is that a team will start to believe that they are focused on the wrong things or that their beliefs and values are not helping to move them forward. Foolish leaders assume though that division among the group is inherently bad. Emotions like envy or anger and a desire for change can benefit the group and a disruptive leader knows how to tame these and use them to the team's advantage.

Disruptive leaders are not manipulative. Their compassion for the work and empathy for the team makes them kind. However, they are not afraid to help the team help itself. Leader's must remain objective and work above and beyond the politics of the group to use both the good and the bad as opportunity to coach a team toward its common goal.

The morale of a team can also be affected adversely by ceremonies that become too repetitive or by process that is too reactive to the day to day challenges that weigh down a team. That said, physical and mental activities are still the antidote for teams with low morale. Fear and anger within a team can burn out of control. Team members who are bored and aimless can spread their fears to other members of the team. It is important to give them something to do even when work has yet to be clearly defined.

Strong leaders recognize this and ensure that individual team members are actively engaged in preparing for things to come. The disruptive leader knows what roles the team could play in new or future work. They harness individual skills to pull a team up out of a rut. When intake of new work slows, or existing activities become too repetitive, and stressful, disruptive leaders find opportunity to offer individuals something exciting to do. This might entail training, developing new skills, or even trying to solve a small but exciting new problem that could benefit the whole group.

Teams at work that are engaged in monotonous or dull activities can suffer the same fate as a team that feels held back by the chaos of a situation. When work is chaotic or dull, team members start to feel not just held back but inferior, alone, or even deserted. Those feelings stem from a lack of security and protection from the hostile or un-wanted environment that an individual can find themselves in. This lack of a more engaging or challenging environment can eventually cause individual team members to reach a breaking point.

Leaders who sense this anxiety will often divert the attention of the team. The best way to distract individuals from the stress or boredom of a working environment is to challenge them with a new situation. Providing the team with mental and physical activities that are new or different can also serve as an outlet for the team's frustration.

The anxiety of a team can be reduced when individuals are given room to navigate problems. However, great leaders know that it's important to coach the team so that they see their situation differently. These leaders would argue that if you don't like the conversation, change it. The disruptive leader doesn't accept complaints at face value. They recognize the need to be objective and look at how all sides may perceive a situation to help bring the team back together. They quickly re-orient the team to solve its own problems or look at a situation differently. By encouraging team members to attack a stressful situation with a new perspective, the disruptive leader gains the trust of the team members and partners who can ultimately help change the conditions.

Again though, these methods work only when the leader is strong enough to remain objective in their thinking. Leaders can't allow themselves to fall into the same hopelessness or lull as the team. Leaders live by example and re-enforce the behaviors and norms of the team. If the leader loses hope, then so will the team. Simple, transparent, and unemotional actions from a leader can instill both confidence and a sense of security among the team.

Looking at things differently is much harder for a team that has worked together longer. As a team matures, people often execute tasks in close order. They mass together and assimilate into a more common and conservative cultural existence. They also commoditize their working relationships and output at-scale. In other words, teams get better at what they do, bigger, and more focused over time. However, along the fringe, small rebellious groups, bored with every day activities, will form. The views of these individuals will branch out and reach toward a new horizon. This behavior will test the boundaries of a team's norms.

The team's focus on a common objective is then constantly at risk when small groups form to test the boundaries of new and more promising opportunities for a team. Disruption always comes knocking and eventually scatters or segments the most mature and stable of organizations in due time. When this happens, teams often struggle to come to grips with an evolving situation.

The masses turn to smaller more adaptable teams for answers. Sometimes they even look for individual contributors to bring order to the chaos. Within the small team or among the individual contributors, it is the psychological reaction of the individual that is more important than emotions are at an aggregate.

Good leaders understand all of this and they learn to play on team member emotions. Disruptive leaders can take advantage of loyalty, courage, vanity, humor, and community. These leaders know the strength and weakness of their team and they use this as an opportunity to build confidence and trust.

When the situation is depressing for one reason or another, a leader can identify a goal that requires action and attention as a distraction. Sometimes when a team is distracted by tasks that keep them busy they will forget about the circumstances they find themselves in. Teams don't always want to control every aspect of the situation. Leaders who try to control everything around them will eventually lose focus. Distracting everyone from certain conditions in the environment is one way to avoid distraction. This tactic can also work to improve morale when a team finds itself bored or about to face a difficult situation. Disruptive leaders also know how to take personal action and in turn do something that removes tension so that the team once again feels safe.

Teams must maintain a competitive edge all the time to remain effective. It isn't enough to just conduct research, discovery, and assessment. They must also have a point of view. Working on or focusing on a certain objective for too long without a mental break or an opportunity to think objectively in the context of a much larger situation can erode a team's effectiveness. Disruptive leaders stress the need for thought leadership on the team. There are three core tenets that successful teams follow when establishing thought leadership.

1. Direction
2. Control
3. Differentiation

Direction means that the team's point of view on a topic of interest should be well organized and guided by the fact that there is a certain niche where their combined craft or skills are most relevant. Control means that thought leadership should exist to re-enforce something and add confidence or security to the team's existing point of view. A point of view should seek to create efficiency and value. Differentiation means that thought leadership should always have some unique qualities that help a team operate with an unexpected or more valuable positioning.

Direction should be tightly focused. Teams should not let thought leadership consume or distract them from other work. Individuals should spark thought leadership on the team by encouraging team members to focus on things they already know as a starting point. Use known aspects of a situation to establish a hypothesis that could be proven or at least explored with the intent of enhancing the common understanding on the team. Using something the team knows and is already good at as a starting point will help to prevent individuals from getting lost or sucked into the exploration of emerging thought.

The control side of a team's point of view should seek to enable repetition, re-use, or find other efficiencies. When a team standardizes things that they do every day, a leader is left to exploit efficiency by identifying re-usable resources that could accelerate new work or create more partnership. Leaders should ensure that team members working on thought leadership are "fresh" and not burned out. This will ensure that they see the control side of the equation more objectively.

Sometimes, teams that are burned out, tired, and just coming out of a previous work effort may not be able to see a situation objectively enough. They can't identify re-use or repetition. They will also miss the point of focusing on something they have experiences in. Good leaders should recognize and understand this before assigning individuals to work that involves thought leadership.

If possible, leaders should also look to take advantage of work that was done for other purposes as a way of harvesting a point of view in an efficient manner. Sometimes, a tremendous amount of value can be unlocked by just tapping into or mining a team's resources for another cause. Every team has waste and inefficiency. Just looking at this waste and re-imagining what it could be used for is often an exciting way to re-think a team's common interests in a new light.

Differentiation requires a very responsible and intelligent leader. The disruptive leader seeks truth and understanding. They don't resort to rhetoric or use dialog and thought leadership as a power move in conversation. These leaders value philosophy and objective thought over the exchange of value for personal gain and influence. In other words, one's own thought leadership and influence are not a means to win an argument.

Instead, thinking is a way of seeking or finding truth and enlightenment about a subject. Therefore, differentiation of thought is the natural end state of understanding the unique circumstances a leader or team is facing. It is also the most difficult way to develop a point of view because it does require deep cognitive reasoning and reflection. All too often, teams will simply repeat what they have read or heard without stopping to really think through their own experience or gut reaction to understand how this might reflect on the situation at hand.

A team can still have a point of view and be considered a thought leader, even if they haven't necessarily distinguished themselves among others inside or outside of an organization. For example, an audience may choose to recognize a team's output or contribution as significant. Leaders may have done very little to encourage or communicate the thought leadership of a team. Yet, various audiences may adopt some of the team's ideas. In this way, a team's success or perspective could still gain widespread attention for its novelty.

True differentiation is a goal that is rarely realized, but, when it is, it can be disruptive for a team. Finding the angle that sets a point of view apart from others is difficult and hard to quantify or even prioritize. Strong leaders recognize that the outcome of thought leadership is only as good as the resources they have assembled and the goals they have focused on. Without the right people and the right goal, differentiation can't be achieved. In other words, "garbage in" is more often "garbage out".

The team's objectives will naturally push thought leaders in a common direction. Leaders also help to focus these individuals. The disruptive leader will find a way to paint a broader brush across the canvas to cover edge cases that could be hiding opportunity. This means that teams must learn to explore connected areas that are not directly relevant. Creativity and inspiration require exposure. Great ideas are a bit like a flower and disruptive leaders are a lot like the bees that cross-pollinate them. These leaders expose themselves to a wide variety of ideas and cross-pollinate them in unlikely places. Disruptive leaders are great explorers, but they are equally good at making sure the team isn't wandering too far off a given path.

The most competent team members and leaders are often held in reserve to help pull together and weave the story as things emerge. They recognize that thought leadership is a valuable commodity. In the end, it must be protected as intellectual capital yet shared to influence or establish awareness of a team's ability.

Small yet highly motivated and determined teams can have an overwhelmingly decisive impact on a situation. Time and time again, teams that lack resources overcome the odds with courage and resolution. Even the smallest of groups can influence sudden change in a situation through thought leadership, tenacity, or optimism. The actions of individuals on these teams can appear miraculous despite a seemingly small number of resources.

Work is just that, it is work, which means that it isn't always easy. Sometimes, when the pressure is high, and the organization is in crisis, the smallest of actions can move the tide one way or another. Those on the other side of the work, whether they are customers or competitors, have their own challenges and frustrations. It's hard to really understand what may be happening on the outside. Even a team that feels like it is failing or in crisis could be producing output that is favorable. Even the slightest extra effort by a team could end up decisive.

In the age of analytics and numbers, one will find that it isn't always the best idea that wins or even the best results for that matter. Miracles can happen when a more determined group solves a problem and tells a better story with not a lot to back it up. The team's solution to the problem may not be the right solution or worse yet it may not even be a quality solution, yet, it wins the day. Sometimes the psychological effect of something is decisive. A few efficient and resolute actions can result in a miracle.

That said, disruptive leaders understand that their strongest players are of utmost value to the team. If they lose these individuals, the loss can have an exponential impact on the morale of the group. An entire team can lose its will and determination when they lose individuals that the team feels are of utmost value.

Great leaders recognize that miracles can sow the seeds of victory. It is the strong leader and a few great individuals that can shape the outcome and chances of success for a team.

Great leaders are optimistic and tenacious despite a wave of negative energy thrown at a team. Positive thinking is difficult to maintain and is easily eroded over time. Teams will cycle through new people, confusion will occur as the situation changes, risks will turn into challenges, failure will be discussed, and reports will exaggerate the situation. These things eat away at a leader's ability to remain determined. That said, disruptive leaders resist the onslaught and stay focused and overly optimistic. Otherwise, the leader and the team will become bogged down in discouragement and despair.

Tenacity requires a relentless pursuit of a goal. Tenacity though is not to be confused with the vicious nature of a bulldog when pursuing a given course of action. Great leaders recognize when a change in methods is perhaps more desirable for a given audience. The team must maintain a strong and adaptable spirit without pig headedness and stupidity. Through endurance, a disruptive leader can accept the conditions of a situation and remain determined to coach the team toward its goals.

A leader's weakness is reflected in the team. The reverse is also true. The weakness of a team and its lack of "determination and will" reflects the spirit of its leadership.

Disruptive leaders rarely believe or take for face value the reports they are given. Especially when information is pessimistic. They want to see first-hand and understand more. These leaders understand the contradiction that failure and success can indeed be the same thing. When they are confronted with reports of failure they question them and objectively re-imagine information in a more optimistic light. Again though, these leaders are not foolish, or pig headed, they, in fact, recognize that there is still value in pessimistic information. These leaders usually see triggers or red flags in a report quickly. The disruptive leader can connect the dots and use information like this to their advantage.

Teams that accept pessimistic reports or information at full value all too often fail. A disruptive leader will recognize this and impress upon everyone a sense of resolve toward the team's goals and objectives. In this way, tenacity and optimism are contagious. Leaders can spread them to the hearts of others and impress upon the team a desire to win.

ABOUT THE AUTHOR

Joe Boroi is a technologist with more than 15 years of proven leadership experience. This project was inspired by a comparison of our modern world to a post-industrial one. Joe has lead teams of analysts, scientists, user experience researchers, visual designers, architects, and software developers. He has helped organizations around the world with product development, integration, digital transformation, organizational maturity, commercialization, and enablement strategy. He is also a former military officer, that served as a platoon leader in both a tank battalion and mechanized infantry regiment. He currently resides in Columbus, Ohio.